India's Emerging Partnerships in Eurasia:

Strategies of New Regionalism

India's Emerging Partnerships in Eurasia:

Strategies of New Regionalism

Nivedita Das Kundu

Vij Books India Pvt Ltd

New Delhi (India)

Published by

Vij Books India Pvt Ltd
(Publishers, Distributors & Importers)
2/19, Ansari Road
Delhi – 110 002
Phones: 91-11-43596460, 91-11-47340674
Fax: 91-11-47340674
e-mail: vijbooks@rediffmail.com

Copyright © 2016, *Nivedita Das Kundu*

ISBN   : 978-93-85563-65-2 (Hardback)
ISBN   : 978-93-85563-66-9 (ebook)

This book is dedicated to my husband Sameer and my sons Shreenik and Arjunaditya

Contents

Preface

This Book is a part of the research project conducted under the auspicious of the Center for Joint Warfare Studies (CENJOWS) and United Service Institution of India (USI). This study unravels the discourse prevailing on the Emerging Partnerships between India and the Eurasian States is framed under the label of new regionalism. The broad aims and objective of this Book is to investigate into Eurasia's relevance for India and its significance in the regional/international power politics and economics. The general discourse is that in the 21st century, Eurasia's geopolitical relevance is on rise. The region has major stakes in the geopolitics of oil and gas, security issues, climate change and power dynamics of major states. The study tried to explore the historical linkages, focusing on the institutional connections, highlighting the policies that underpin such region-building approaches.

This study is considerably based on field work and primary source materials collected from the countries concerned. While conducting this research the study adopted various tools, like interviews taken from relevant academics, policy makers and strategic analysts, served as an important source of information for providing perspectives both in terms of facts and documents. The range of the respondent types was substantially large, thus, making the study more objective and empirical. Relevant information was also gathered from various government reports, books, research papers and local newspaper articles, etc. Efforts were made to enlist the help of Central Asian, Russian, South Caucasian as well as Indian scholars and bureaucrats to the advantage of data collection and perspective building. Though considerable quantitative data was gathered the essential thrust of the research was made through the qualitative technique and methodology used was historical and analytical in nature.

The **Introduction** outlines the objective of this Book focussing on the significance of Eurasian states for India in the regional framework as well as in the context of international power politics and economics. **Chapter 1,** is on the **Geostrategic Significance and Bilateral Relations** focuses on India and the Eurasian states of Russia, Central Asia and South Caucasus close ties that have been continuing over the period of time in number of spheres. However, there are still many glaring weaknesses in India's policy and approach towards the region. India and the countries of Eurasia i.e. Russia, Central Asia and Caucasus are determined to strengthen the cooperation matching with the historical connections in the contemporary era. However, there is a need to review and re-energise its efforts to manage the new set of challenges, to ensure the security and to improve the connectivity with each other. **Chapter 2,** examines the **Silk Route Connectivity and the Regional Transport Corridors,** this chapter examines the revival of ancient *Silk Route* connectivity for improving the linkages that could increase the regional cooperation and can be considered as a major tool for transport and trade developments. This Chapter emphasises that there are major markets that surrounds these land-locked countries of Eurasia, can be connected easily through viable routes as these linkages are expected to increase the regional cooperation and can be considered as a major tool for transport and trade developments. **Chapter 3,** discusses on the **Energy Security and the Development Strategies**, this chapter stresses on India and the Eurasian States need for greater and more focused attention for the security concerns, on the energy issues as well as on the development strategies in its policies. **Chapter 4,** focuses on the **Network Diplomacy and the Rise of New Regional Organisations,** this Chapter also highlights that India and the Eurasian states need to move towards a strategic vision for building the missing Asian architecture. In this Chapter it has been accentuated that India and the Eurasian countries of former Soviet States can work closely to use all existing and nascent regional initiatives such as SCO, BRICS, RIC, CICA, CAREC, EurAsEC, Customs Union, Eurasian Union etc. for strengthening cooperation with each other. This book also provides **Recommendations** and **Future Scenarios** to widen perspectives and explore uncertain aspects of the future to formulate policies and look for new opportunities in the regional framework.

The research queries addressed and highlighted in the Chapters of this book articulate contours of India's relations with the Eurasian states; the readers will find important information that the volume tried to unleash giving new perspectives. The empirical and objective findings of the study would provide impetus to various stakeholders involved in the process of policy making. Thus, besides contributing to the existing academic knowledge, the purpose of this Book is also to provide inputs into foreign policy decision making.

— **Nivedita Das Kundu**

Acknowledgement

I would like to convey my gratitude to the United Service Institutions of India (USI), New Delhi, and Center for Joint Warfare Studies (CENJOWS) New Delhi, for permitting me to undertake this research work and provided support, encouragement and guidance.

I thank my colleagues in India and abroad for their meaningful input and cooperation. I am also thankful to the staff of Lenin's Library in Russia, Library of the University of Toronto, Library of York University, Library of Congress, Foreign Ministry of Turkmenistan, United Ataturk Alatoo University Kyrgyzstan, Center for Strategic Studies, Azerbaijan, Baku, United Service Institutions of India's library, Jawaharlal Nehru University Library in India.

I would like to thank my family members who helped me and encouraged me to complete this Book.

It is entirely due to the whole hearted cooperation, assistance of all the persons and Institutes mentioned above that this book has taken shape. Needless to say, the faults and aberrations are entirely my own.

— *Nivedita Das Kundu*

Abbreviations

ADB	Asian Development Bank
ALTID	Asian Land Transport Infrastructure Development
BAM	Baikal-Amur Mainline
BRICS	Brazil-Russia-India-China
BSES	Black Sea Economic Cooperation
BTC	Baku-Tbilisi-Ceyhan
CAREC	Central Asian Regional Economic Cooperation
CARs	Central Asian Republics
CCIT	Comprehensive Convention on International Terrorism
CECA	Comprehensive Economic Cooperation Agreement
CEPA	Comprehensive Economic Partnership Agreement
CICA	Conference on Interaction and Confidence Building Measures in Asia
CIS	Commonwealth of Independent States
CIS	Commonwealth of Independent States
CSTO	Collective Security Treaty Organisation
DMIC	Delhi-Mumbai Industrial Corridor
EBRD	European Bank for Reconstruction and Development
EEU	Eurasian Economic Union
EurAsEC	Eurasian Economic Community

FGFA	Fifth Generation Fighter Aircraft
FSU	Former Soviet Union
GAIL	Gas authority of India limited
HAL	Hindustan Aeronautics Limited
IEP	Integrated Energy Policy
IGC	Inter-Governmental Commission
IMU	Islamic Movement of Uzbekistan
INSTC	International North South Transport Corridor
ITEC	Indian Technical and Economic Cooperation Programme
MTU	Metric tons uranium
ONGC	Oil and Natural gas Company
OSCE	Organization for Security and Cooperation in Europe
OVL	ONGC Videsh Ltd
PSUs	Public Sector Units
RATS	Regional Anti-Terrorist Structure
RCTS	Regional Counter Terrorist Structure
RFSS	Russian Federal Security Service
RIC	Russia-India-China
SCO	Shanghai Cooperation Orgnisation
TAPI	Turkmenistan–Afghanistan–Pakistan–India
TNOC	transnational oil corporations
TRACECA	Transport Corridor for Europe-Caucasus-Asia
TSR	Trans-Siberian Railway
UNDP	United Nations Development Programme
UNESCO	United Nations Educational, Scientific and Cultural Organization
WMD	Weapons of mass destruction

Introduction

The discourse on the emerging Partnerships between India and the Eurasian States is framed under the label of new regionalism. This discourse has tended to explore the historical linkages, institutions, policies and economic relations that underpin such region-building approaches. This book attempts to focus on India's ancient linkages, connectivity as well as the proximity with the States of the Eurasian region providing the regional perspective. The book also tries to describe and debate various aspects providing historical background, literary discourses and the present dynamics of the region.

Eurasia is a vast land mass of the territory extending from the Caspian to the western China and the area stretching from the Urals to the Great Mountain Arc in the west formed by the Altai, Tien Shan, the Pamir, the Hindukush and the kopet Dagh running through the Vast steppes and deserts covering the whole region.[1] Russia, Central Asia and the Caucasus states cover this great Eurasian land mass. The immediate neighbours of these Eurasian states are the Xinjiang region of China, Mongolia, Afghanistan and also the North-west region of pre-independence India.[2] Due to the close proximity, ethno-cultural ties, it was even thought once to include all these neighbouring states into the Eurasian States and bring them under the common regional structure. There are evidences which depict the fact that close cultural, religious and economic ties existed between India and Eurasia from the very early times. The terminology Eurasia is also used in international politics as a neutral way to refer to the post-Soviet States. However,

Eurasia as a distinct geo-cultural space not entirely separated from Europe but functioning as a contradistinction of the conventional paradigms of 'east' and 'west'.

The idea of Eurasia as per Alexandr Dugin, "Eurasia does not have fixed boundaries, Eurasia is a civilizational structure, it is a geopolitical connotation". The term Eurasia or *Evraziia* was used by Eurasianist sometimes to refer to the 'continent' to specify this mega-region but that usage was for them metaphorical rather than scientific. The Eurasianist move developed in 1920s inside Russian intellectuals who had immigrated to Western Europe after the October Revolution, including Peter N. Savitskii, George Vernadskii and Nikolai Sergeevich Trubetskoi, the ethnographer and philologist. They claimed that the Eurasian continent had served as the arena for the formation and development of a distinct civilization and cultural sphere, a civilization that absorbed and blended both European and Asiatic elements. This vision of the territorial contours of this continent coincided in large measure, with those of the Russian Empire with exception of its western borderlands in Finland, the Baltic regions and Poland. Across these broad spaces, Eurasia was a zone of profound ethnographic diversity made-up of a core of Russians, Ugro-Finnic peoples and Turkic population of the Volga basin and Central Asia. Russia's geographical existence within a larger zone of Eurasian civilization meant that Russian culture had been shaped to an insignificant extent by influences coming from Asia, this connotation was also used by Nikolas Trubetskoi used. Referring to a wide historical array of manifestations of Russian culture, he emphasized the preeminent importance of connections to the east as compared to those of the west. He argued that the Russians, Ugro-Finns and Volga Turks comprise of a cultural zone that has connections with both the Slavs and the Turianian East and that it was difficult to identify which was more important. He also mentioned that Russian's were Eurasian and not European, not only by virtue of their cultural patterns but in terms of anthropological-racial consideration as well. He mentioned in his writings that, Turkic blood mingles in Russian veins with that of Ugro-Finns and the Slavs. As per his narration it is usually forgotten that, if not in language or faith, but in blood, character and culture, Russian's are not only the Slavs but the Turanians too.

Mark Bass argued that Trubetskoi's ideas on the implications of Eurasia's geographic character were ultimately intended to prepare a new conceptual ground to support the need to maintain the unity and integrity of the historic spaces of the Eurasian state. Bassin further argued that trubetskoi's position of Russia-Eurasia has to be understood in the context of post-war European and trans-Atlantic discourse of self-determination. He explicitly associated Russia with the colonial real's of the non-European world with a view for appropriating post-revolutionary Russia with the same principles and standards that were later on being accorded to other post-colonial regions. Bassin argues that Tubetskoi replaced imperial Russia with the alternative of Eurasia as the legitimate repository of the national sovereignty of all groups across the continental expanse. He noted that, by virtue of the pluralism of ethnic groups, Eurasia was a 'peculiar' type of nation and the development of a pan-Eurasian nationalism was necessary to provide a sense of unity necessary for a viable state. This 'peculiar multi-ethnic state,' possessing its own nationalism called as Eurasian, the territory is known as Eurasia and its nationalism as Eurasianism.

Today, there is a need to take note that the Eurasian debate itself is not a monolithic on the whole and in its various forms serves distinct purposes. What seems to be emerging in multiple visions where each region has its own perspectives. However, the idea of 'Eurasia' is also providing an arena for new geo-political relations to be formed between the regional players. Caroline Humphrey mentioned in her work that Eurasia is likely to be highly influential both in conceptualizing federal relations and in shaping the political-cultural character of the constituent regions. However, it is important to take into account the whole region together and include all those who have occupied this vast space.

In the contemporary geographic definition, the intra-continental space of Eurasia is understood to constitute of the Five Central Asian Republics, Afghanistan; the four Slavic states of Russia, Belorussia, Ukraine and Moldavia; the three Caucasian states of Azerbaijan, Georgia and Armenia; and the three Baltic states of Estonia, Latvia and Lithuania. However, the study of this Volume focuses on the strategically located resource-rich Eurasian region came into prominence mainly after the collapse of the Soviet Union, when these states became independent sovereign states. Radical Islamist extremist activities emanating from the region also put the region in global spotlight, especially after 9/11 attacks.[3] Today, Eurasian states are occupying an increasingly crucial place in the international power politics. These nations are at varying stages of political or economic development. Some are vibrant democracies whereas; others are still following centralized regimes. They have not had the opportunity to develop a defined culture for strategic and security planning or for policy engineering. Furthermore, these newly independent states tend to underestimate certain security threats, exaggerate others and sometimes even overlooked vital factors in national security planning. Their strategic visions and calculations are mainly based on historical events with reference to ethnic lines.

Eurasia's geo-strategic location makes the region a focal point for foreign powers as well as potential conflict between them. The US, EU, China, Japan, Pakistan, Saudi Arabia, and Israel are all interested in the region. It can thus be said that here a 'New Great Game' is underway. Unlike the 'Great Game' of the nineteenth century, which was played out between the British Empire and the Czarist Russia, the post-Cold War 'Great Game' involves not only states but also non-state actors, international organizations, transnational oil corporations (TNOCs) etc. are active in the region. Amoung others "The Organization for Security and Cooperation in Europe", (OSCE) is also active in the region. For India, Eurasian states are situated in its extended neighbourhood. Driven by India's security concerns and increasing energy needs, India shows deep interest in the region and maintains close and cooperative relationship.

This Book discuses about India's relationship and engagement with the Eurasian states focusing mainly on India's close linkages and cooperation with Russia, Central Asia and with the South Caucasus in various spheres. India shows deep interest in the region and maintains relatively high profile because of its long-standing special relationship with these states and due to its age-old trade and economic links through the silk route connections.

It is well known fact that people of this region interacted with the people of India, intermingled and influenced each other since the very dawn of history. The mountain barriers that separate the two regions could not become an insurmountable barrier. The powerful spiritual cultural upsurge and intellectual ferment in one region have tended to spread over the other side of the mountainous divide. Buddhism spread from India to the Eurasian region and a rich Indo-Islamic composite culture spread from that region to India in the medieval period. The name of Al Beruni (11th century) from the Khorezm region of present-day Uzbekistan stands out as the most prominent Central Asia scholar of India in the medieval period. He mentioned in his work many such commonalities and connectivity.

The similarities between these states and India can be traced from the time when stone tools discovered in the North Indian Territory of Punjab and Kashmir; these tools were excavated in the cities of Gissar culture in Tajikistan. Also, Ceramics from Harappa, Lazurites seals and fragments have been found in the tributary of Amudarya in Tajikistan and in the Southern Bank of River Pyanj.

The archival data mentions that the Harappan settlements received the supply of Lazurites from the mines of Badakhshan in the Pamir region of the Tajikistan area. The trade and economic linkages could be traced by the remnants discovered in the Altyn-Tepe in Turkmenistan and in Shortugai in Tajikistan, which clearly depicts the close trade and economic ties, which continued through the art and handicraft products between Central Asian States and the North West Indian states.

During the IInd and the IIIrd millennium BC, ancient connections were strengthened further when the migration from India and Central Asian states to this region continued in full swing. The Kushan and the Mughal Empires are the well known historical connections between India and the Eurasian region. India's contact with the Central Asian states could be traced also during Emperor Ashoka's period, as his empire extended upto the borders of that region. The archival data also mentioned that the trace of different rulers of the Central Asian Scythians, Huns and the Sakas were found, who all even ruled in the North-Western part of India.

India's connection with the Eurasian state of Russia is also very old. The close connections between them were found in the cultural connectivity as well as through the mythological linkages. Many similarities were traced between the Slavs and the Indians mainly due to their close connectivity as a neighbour in the common territory for a longer period. It has also been observed that among the Indo-European language, Sanskrit language is very similar to the Russian language. As far as Russian language's grammatical rules and syntax are concerned, they strictly follow the great Indian Scholar and a grammar specialist Panini's theory (during the VIth Century BC). Also, the traces of common connectivity were found in the work of eminent Indian scholar and well known statesman B.G. Tilak's work. In his work "The Arctic home in the Vedas", he has depicted the closeness between the Indo-Aryans and Russian

Slavs by providing the evidence which could be traced through the religion, language, & mythology, that was mainly possible due to their close habitat and close proximity to each other. According to Tilak the Vedas were composed in the Arctic region in the inter-glacial period. He also mentioned in his work about 'Airiana Vaejo', which means 'Aryan Paradise'.⁴Many Indian and Russian Scholars provided evidence which clearly stated that the ancestors of the Slavs and the Indo-Aryans stayed in the northern Russian region from where one group migrated to India through Central Asian States and Afghanistan and the other group migrated towards the Western direction. A famous Russian historian A. Asov mentioned in his work that thousands of years before the 'Kiev-Rus', existed, a 'Vedic Rus' was professing in Russian Vedas. This pre-Christian ancient 'Rus', was characterized by him as a national variant of the international Vedic culture of which the 'Avestian' and 'Vedic Indian cultures', are the two significant components.

A Book titled 'Rus Vedicheskaya', authored by Yu.V. & Yu.G. Mizyn which published in Moscow in the year 2004 mentions that their ancestors came from North, descending upon the Urals and the steppes in the Semirechie region and from there to India and Iran. During 14th Century, Indian gold coins were found in the Volga region near a village called Tenishevo, thus, indicating a flourishing trade. In fact, a trade route between India and Russia had existed through Central Asia and the Caspian Sea since X^{th}-XIth Centuries. There existed rich trade in Kashmiri Shawls, which Indian Traders carried to distant Eurasian region. There were even arguments among scholars over naming the trade route from Kashmir-Central Asia-Xinjiang to Russia as the 'Shawl Route', instead of 'Silk Route'. There still exists a temple called Ateshgha temple (the fire temple) in Azerbaijan near Baku, which was constructed on the mid-way of the trading route and was regularly visited by Indian pilgrims throughout the 19ᵗʰ Century. Even today, many "Saraies" (motels) are preserved carefully in Baku which was originally built by the traders while travelling through the 'Silk

Route'. The remnants of the Armenian trading posts and churches still exist in the Indian City of Kolkata and Chennai.

British Colonial power was conscious of the Indian historical linkages with the Eurasian states and did not hesitate to promote its strategic and geopolitical goals through these connections. During the World War I, a contingent of Indian soldiers was even sent under the leadership of General Malleson based in Iran, with the aim of preventing Baku's oil fields from the German hands. British Indian authorities continued the military actions in Central Asia and in the South-Caucasian states even after the World War I. The British however, failed to turn the scale against the Bolsheviks in the Civil War following the 1917 October revolution in Russia. However, the Malleson expedition, the Bailey mission to Tashkent and the mission of Col. Etherton to Kashgar points to the failed Britishers efforts to involve colonial India into the "Great Game" of the region. However, in the recent period the revival of the "New Great Game", which has started in the region mainly due to the hydrocarbon and mineral resources has the potential to destabilize the region creating new problems and security threats which needs to be addressed with the close regional cooperation.

Common religious bondings have also helped to get India closer to the Eurasian states. It has been mentioned in the archival reports that the traces have been found that Buddhism started to spread in Eurasia from the beginning of the new era. There were two important centers of the early Indian Buddhist influence in Eurasia and these were in the Eastern Turkistan and in Afghanistan. The nation of Tokharians played significant role in the spread of Buddhism. Buddhism entered in Bactria to Kharistan during the reign of Kanishka the first. During the era of the highest powers of the Kushan state (IInd and IVth Centuries AD), when its capital was located near modern Peshawar in Pakistan, Buddhist Communities spread their influence deep into the valley of Surhandari river. It was during this time when the famous Buddha statues in Bamyan region of Afghanistan were excavated. After the defeat of the Kushans by Sassanid Iran, Buddhism continued to maintain its influence in Merv (mordern day Mary in Turkmenistan) where Buddhist Monuments were built during the IVth-VIth Centuries. The considerable numbers of Buddhist monuments in the Kara Kum Desert near the Caspian Sea emphasizes the fact that the Buddhist community enjoyed relatively high influence during that time. Buddhist culture also influenced Mongolian, Turkish and many others in the region who all become acquainted with the Buddhist religion, which spread beyond the Indian sub-continent and allowed to bring the countries of the region closer to each other.[5]

In the recent years the revival of the Eurasian geopolitical activities has become prominent and the nationalist and well known scholars are actively engaged in popularizing this idea of Eurasianism and Eurasian connection in the region. Many of them have been collaborating closely with the geopolitical committee of the state Duma supporting the idea for increasing the cooperation even under the RIC, (Russia, India, China,) BRICS (Brazil-Russia-India-China) and SCO forums (Shanghai Cooperation Organisation). Hence, it is important for all the states in the region to engage in close consultation with each other and try to maintain the rich potential and cultural heritage and make the region as a great hub for regional as well as global stability and prosperity.[6]This will be possible by creating a new edifice of peaceful regional cooperation and regional security through non-military approach, maintaining a close contact with each other as well as with the multilateral & international actors having legitimate interest in the region.

Historically embedded yet ongoing Indian ties until the end of the cold war continued peacefully with the Eurasian states. Indian Governments developed increasingly intimate relationship with the former Soviet Union. The Indo-Soviet partnership was highly complementary; it involved energy and arms supplies for India, as well as Science and technological and trade and economic cooperation too. This relationship laid the groundwork for the post-cold war developmental cooperation as well.

Commercial ties between India and Eurasian states are also long-standing and synergetic with cultural connections. Indian ivory, sugar, dies and carpets all were traditionally in great demand in the Eurasian Region. Indians were also major traders and moneylenders along the silk route, together with Parthians and Sogdians many Indians reportedly also lived permanently in the Eurasian states by the middle of the nineteenth century. Trade also flourished between the two regions hence, the southern branch of the historic 'silk route' that connected India with this region was often called the 'cotton and precious goods route'.[7]

The newly won independence, has thrown up new and myriad challenges to the states of Eurasia. They have chosen democratic paradigm to guide their politics and societies. This shift involves intense changes in political and bureaucratic structures including mindsets to steer their nations toward new directions. The new political and constitutional frameworks adopted by these states have raised the expectations of their people who are eager to restore and assert their historical identities. Thus, in search of their national self-identities, the people in these states are keen to look into their glorious past; indentify their national interest and look forward to renew the old linkages. They are also keen to carry forward their cooperation in all possible spheres with other regional players so that geo-economics can prevail over the geo-politics.

The objective of this Book is to focus on the significance of Eurasian states for India in the regional framework as well as in the context of international power politics and economics. While dealing with the topic of India's emerging partnership with the States of Eurasia, it is essential to examine its historical linkages, geopolitical significance, and economic perspective. The major question that comes up while working on the topic is that, can India play a significant role in the region? What factors are working in India's favour in the region? What are the constraints? To what extend can India be seen as a partners with Eurasian States? What strategy can India devise to engage these countries meaningfully and effectively? It has been argued that the states of Eurasia are occupying a central place in the international and regional politics and is also a significant factor for connecting East with the West. This research work attempts to provide a meaningful and a critical contribution in comprehending the bilateral and multilateral relationship between India and the Eurasian states focusing mainly on India's relations with Russia, Central Asia and South Caucasus region and by looking into the possible energy cooperation, transport linkages and the security concerns emanating from the region. It needs to be recognized that these states have emerged from the shadow of socialism and have suffered a totalitarian system for almost about a century. During this period the societies of these Republics witnessed the obliteration of their culture, languages and social structures at massive level. The key idea behind this book is to bring forth the insights, which help in understanding the new geo-political reality and security dynamics and possible regional cooperation. The book has four main chapters besides introduction and conclusion. These chapters specifically addresses issues like geopolitical significance and bilateral relations, silk route connectivity and the regional corridors, energy security and development strategies and network diplomacy and the rise of new regional organisations. This book also tries to provide recommendations and future scenarios.

End Notes

1   Baldwin, 1997, p. 13

2   Chakravarty K.K., "Culture as an Engine for Eurasian Peace and Cooperation", in Bandey A Aijaz ed. *Silk Route and Eurasia: Peace and Cooperation,* Prince Art Printers, New Delhi 2011, pp.119-121.

3   Togan Isenbike, "Twenty Years After : New Histories Emerging", in Sengupta Anita, Chatterjee Suchandana, Sushmita Bhattacharya, ed. *Eurasia Twenty Years After,* Shipra Publishers 2012, pp.53-61

4   Devendra Kaushik lecture given on Eurasia and India, on 11th November at ICSSR, New Delhi

5   Baatr U Kitinov, Conference Paper, *Indian Buddhist Heritage in Central Asia and Eurasia,* 15[2h] November, 2014, New Delhi)

6   Valdai Club 10th anniversary meeting discussions, Valdai, Russia, on 9th September 2014

7   Jyotsna Bakshi *Russia and India: From Ideology to Geopolitics,* Delhi: Dev Publication, 1999, pp. 207–18.

1

Geostrategic Significance and Bilateral Relations

The geo-political importance of Eurasia is indeed immense. Historically, the Eurasian heartland has been considered as a Central strategic area and much of the dramatic events of history have in fact unraveled this political and economic space. After the dissolution of USSR in 1991, the whole edifice of relations built up over decades was severely affected. India and the Former Soviet States drifted apart in the 1990s because of different priorities. While all the newly independent states of Former Soviet Union (FSU) and Russia struggled to cope with the wrenching shift from a state-controlled economy to a free market economy and from a centralized authoritarian regime to a multi-party democracy. During same time India too embarked on a process of economic reforms. Military cooperation between Russia and India were disrupted badly as many defence establishments in the integrated Soviet military industrial corporation were shut down, increased the prices due to lack of coordinated supplies with other defence manufacturing units sprawled all over the post-soviet space. Neither India nor these countries of Eurasian region could devote much time to learn how to deal with the vastly changed circumstances. Political relations too got effected in the early 1990's as during that period the leadership of the newly independent Eurasian states was obsessed with the west and also the foreign policy concerns were to concentrate mainly on the immediate neighborhood. Russia also wanted to regain its political and economic primacy in its near abroad and was busy in curbing instability that was prevailing.

In the early twentieth century, Britain's geopolitical theorist Halford J. Mackinder called Central Eurasia the Eurasian 'Heartland' to highlight the region's geopolitical and geo-strategic importance in global politics. Mackinder opined that the one who would control this region would also control the whole world. Indeed, with the end of the Cold War and disintegration of the Soviet Union, Eurasian region has developed as an important geo-strategic region in world politics.[1]Though, some of the Eurasian States suffered from localized conflicts as well as economic distress. Ethnic tensions continue in many of these states, making the region susceptible to instability and threatening its political and economic development.

India developed strong political relationships with all the states of the former Soviet space since their independence. Eurasian countries have also valued India's emergence in the global stage even as their own trajectories of growth moved upward and the relationships have benefited from mutually advantageous cooperation. The geo-strategic and economic salience of the region has grown with the discovery of hydrocarbon reserves. This has happily translated into significant prosperity for several countries in the region.[2] Russia and the Countries of the Central Eurasian Region by virtue of the geographical location and vast natural resources, including energy reserves has special significance for India. India no doubt wishes to be a long term partner of Eurasia. India looks forward for bolstering the traditional links and respond to challenges of the future.

The following paragraphs of this chapter debate on the emerging relationship between India and these states. In this chapter an attempt has been made to signify specific factors of the region and also focus on India-Eurasia cooperation in various sectors. This Chapter also provides facts and details which shows how the States of Eurasia are also keen to develop close relationship with India due to their civilizational linkages with India. The argument given here is that there is a clear compatibility between India and these states of Eurasia and both India and these countries are trying to promote cooperation in various sectors based on political understanding and bilateral relationship.

India-Russia Relationship

India-Russia relationship has evolved into an equal partnership. The deep roots of this relationship go back to the early 20th century when India was under British rule and the Czars ruled Russia. The Russian Revolution of 1905 inspired Indian freedom fighters. Mahatma Gandhi was also struck by the similarity in the prevailing conditions in Russia and India. He developed a close connection with Russia and carried on lengthy correspondence with Leo Tolstoy. Russia's communist leader V.I. Lenin followed with interest and sympathy the nascent Indian freedom struggle. Following 1917 Bolshevik Revolution, the Soviet leaders understood that their revolution stood better chance of success and encouraged India to become free and independent. Many Indian freedom fighters who were greatly inspired by the Bolshevik Revolution established personal contacts with the Soviet leaders. It was Pandit Nehru's thinking, which laid foundation of the policy of the Indian National Congress towards the Soviet Union. After visiting Soviet Union in 1927, on the occasion of the 10th anniversary of the Bolshevik Revolution, Jawaharlal Nehru came back deeply impressed with the Soviet experiment. He was convinced that poor developing country like India needed to follow not the capitalist path but a development model that emphasized social justice, equality and human dignity. Nehru was emphatic that India must develop close and friendly relationship with the Soviet Union. It is noteworthy that even before India became independent, an official announcement was made on 13 April 1947 on the establishment of diplomatic relations between India and the Soviet Union.[3]

Nehru's faith in the Soviet Union was immense. The Soviet Union consistently gave India valuable political, diplomatic and strategic support bilaterally as well as in international forums on Kashmir and other vital issues affecting India's national interests. It was Soviet diplomatic backing and material support and the confidence provided by the Indo-Soviet Treaty of Peace, Friendship and Cooperation, which enabled India to successfully undertake the operations in 1971 that led to the creation of Bangladesh. This political understanding was underpinned by a strong economic and strategic relationship. Beginning in the 1950s, India received from the Soviet Union generous assistance for its industrialization as well as for development in the areas of defence, space and atomic energy. Short of capital, foreign exchange and technology, India appreciated the support that it received low-priced economic credits for infrastructure projects repayable in rupees; reliable affordable and good quality military supplies, also on credit and supply of crucial products like oil and oil product, fertilizer, metals etc. mostly via swap deal. Some of India's globally competitive public sector companies like BHEL, Oil and Natural Gas Corporation (ONGC) and Hindustan Aeronautics Limited (HAL), as well as the steel industry in India, were set up with Soviet cooperation. The first Indian Institute of Technology set up with foreign collaboration was the one in Mumbai with the Soviet support.[4] Soviet Union helped India in many ways to become more self-reliant and was a true partner of India.

Today, both India and Russia have acquired a new self-confidence arising out of their rapid economic growth, at the time when many developed countries are suffering from economic recession. As rising economic powers, both India and Russia are playing an increasingly larger role on the world stage. The two countries share the goal of creating multipolar world. India values the political and diplomatic support it continues to get from Russia on vital issues. India is also happy to note that Russia is recovering economically and militarily and is reasserting itself on the international sphere.[5] In today's complicated and fast changing geopolitical situation, both countries have wisely diversified their foreign policy options, yet have been careful not to abandon a mutually beneficial partnership of trust built up over decades.

India-Russia cooperation is going on smoothly and steadily in various sectors. Cooperation in the defence sector is still the strongest link. Even today around 50% of the defence equipment used by the Indian defence forces is of Russian origin. India is cooperating with Russia on major defence projects such as on indigenously developed nuclear submarine Arihant, the Fifth Generation Fighter Aircraft (FGFA). Off late, Russia also participated in the formation of the first group of Indian satellites for distant probing of the earth. The first launch of IRS series satellites was conducted by "Vostok" rocket. Russia has also advanced a proposal for selling the advanced MiG-35 fighter jet to the IAF. A $3.77 billion deal for the supply of 40 SU-30MKI Russian fighter aircraft to India was also signed. The agreements included proposal for procuring around 10,000 'Invar' missiles, T-90 tanks and over 200 air-launched versions of the BrahMos supersonic cruise missiles.[6] Russia still remains India's largest supplier of military equipment despite the entry of US and Israel, which have apparently, also became major suppliers of military hardware to India.

In the nuclear-power sector Russia has already constructed two nuclear power plants at Kudankulam in south of India under Indo-Russian Nuclear Cooperation program. Negotiations for two additional units on the same site are also going on. In the space sector too, India-Russia cooperation on *Glonass* is going on well. India is also trying to get Russian Technology in tracking satellites and to have a collaborative *Chandrayaan* II, project involving space probes to the moon.[7]

Indo-Russian energy cooperation is also expected to get a boost in the coming years. India imports oil, mostly from the volatile region of Middle East. However, to sustain current high rate of growth, India need to secure and diversify sources of energy import. According to the International Energy Agency, India would be the third largest energy consumer in the world by 2025 after US and China.[8]Russia, India's trusted strategic partner is destined to play a vital role in ensuring India's energy security in the coming decades.

The former Soviet Union played a major role in building India's energy sector by building tens of hydropower stations, developing India's coal industry, finding oil in Indian soil and helping in setting up India's energy major ONGC. Indo-Russian energy cooperation acquired new dimensions in the post-Soviet period, particularly in the hydrocarbon and nuclear sector. India has invested $2.8 billion in the Sakhalin energy project, controlling 20% stakes in the venture and has purchased Imperial Energy, (London-listed oil major in Tomks region).[9] These are India's largest investments abroad in energy sector.

India is energy deficient country and Russia is energy surplus and therefore, a mutual interest lies in this sector. Indian side feels that there is a clear compatibility between India's needs and Russia's resources. Indian side is adopting a policy to implement the experience of Sakhalin-1 to other oilfields in Russia.[10] India's policy is to promote the idea of India's willingness to offer Russian companies to participate in Indian oil and gas projects, both upstream and downstream, as well as to undertake joint exploration in other countries too. India has geared-up its energy diplomacy and is moving quickly to penetrate in the Russian energy market.

Today, the weakest link in Indo-Russian cooperation remains trade and economic ties. Trade between the two countries is extremely low[11] Of course, the proposal to increase this target has been announced by both the sides. Now that stringent visa regulations have eased to certain extend, the dynamic private sector companies of both the countries are engaged in boosting-up the economic partnership with each other. Private Sector in both the countries is trying to work closely to give a new direction to the economic relationship.

India and Russia have also been trying to engage each other to boost-up the economic partnership through Comprehensive Economic Partnership Agreement (CEPA). Today Russia is a WTO member and it also has formed Customs Union with Belarus and Kazakhstan to a "Common Economic Space". Therefore, it is expected that CEPA with the broader Eurasian region might come-up soon. It is expected that Russia will also invest in the Delhi-Mumbai Industrial Corridor (DMIC) project. This project covers an area of about 400,000 sq.km and six states with a population of 178 million. This project incorporates nine mega industrial zones.[12]

However, there are still certain issues related to inadequate banking and financial services, lack of brand promotion, removal of discrimination in insurance coverage and quality control concerns are coming-up as a stumbling block in Indo-Russian economic cooperation. The Russian side appreciated that the simplified visa regime for Russian citizens being implemented by the Indian side and this move had contributed to a 24% increase in Russian tourists travelling to India in the year 2011-12 as compared to the earlier years.[13] India and Russia are also trying to collaborate on new areas which need to be explored further, like in the area of democratisation process, social policy diffusion, in religious dialogues, in promoting secularism, tolerance, multi-ethnicity, for developments of internal economic management and planning etc. which are all significant areas for both India and Russia and could be addressed together.

Russia's preference for multipolarity and encouragement for the promotion of groupings like RIC (Russia-India-China), BRICS (Brazil-Russia-India-China-South Africa), as well as SCO (Shanghai Cooperation Organisation) is intended to create a forum outside the Western block where India and Russia along with other countries can discuss issues without western pressure.[14] Amidst all these positive developments as well as certain concerns, there is a hope that India-Russia friendship and the strategic partnership will scale new heights and it will grow, thrive and blossom in the coming years.

Nonetheless, there is a need to create wider public interest and understanding for developing the relationship, particularly among the increasingly influential younger generations. Without strong public support, it will be difficult to provide greater depth, a sound foundation and long-term stability to this mutually beneficial strategic partnership. There is no substitute for spontaneous and natural people-to people exchanges. India and Russia will need to build direct contacts with the entire spectrum of stakeholders and interest groups in the political, economic, military and other spheres. Today, India-Russia relationship has many positive dimensions and can move on steadily. India's connections with other former Soviet States specially with the two distinct parts of Central Eurasia i.e. five states of Central Asia and three States of South Caucasus is also significant and the relationship is developing significantly over the past two decades since these countries got their independence.

India-Central Asia Relationship

In Soviet times the Central Asian region was called *Sredniaia Azia* (Middle Asia). *Sredniaia Azia* includes Kyrgyzstan, Tajikistan, Turkmenistan, Uzbekistan and Kazakhstan. Western scholars mostly use the term 'Central Asia,' while some Russians have not yet dropped the old term 'Middle Asia.' Another term, 'Greater

Central Asia', is of more or less recent coinage.[15] Recently this term has been given more exact geopolitical specification and applied to the five former Soviet Republics including Afghanistan.

The emergence of fifteen independent states as a result of the collapse of the Soviet Union in 1991, has offered new challenges and opportunities for India to broaden its bilateral and multilateral relationships with Central Asian States. Since the Soviet period, India had close relationship with the Five Central Asian States. Though India's close cooperation with these States since the Soviet Union days was indeed an advantage for developing relationship with these post-Soviet newly independent states of Central Asia, however, in the changed situation there was a need to shift its focus from the larger canvas of the Soviet Union to a smaller canvas to renew and build close ties with each of these five new Republics.

Throughout India's history, connectivity with Central Asia has been extremely important. Central Asia has been India's principal door to connect India with Europe. These Countries have deeply influenced India's history, culture and polity. Of all India's neighbouring regions, whether across land or maritime frontiers, it is with Central Asia that India has had the longest association and the most extensive people-to-people ties. Today, Central Asia gets significant priority under India's foreign policy.

India's interests in Central Asia are fundamentally strategic. India always wanted Central Asia to be stable as well as secular. India believes that weak, unstable Central Asia with centrifugal tendencies could become a haven for terrorism, separatism and fundamentalism making the region volatile, as instability in Central Asia carries the danger of a domino effect across the entire region.[16] India is working actively to get a firm foothold in Central Asia, so that this strategically located region does not become an area dominated by forces inimical or hostile to the regions interests. On the economic side, the Central Asian market is relatively small. However, India is trying to gain access to the rich natural resources of the region, such as oil and gas, uranium, rare earths and minerals and also trying to develop defence cooperation.

Fortunately, there are many factors working in India's advantage in Central Asia. India is viewed by Central Asian States as a benign power that does not pose any direct contemporary threat. There is a tremendous cultural attraction and liking that still exists and creates certain romance and mystique for the people of this region. India's 'soft power', which has captivated Central Asia in the past, has the potential to be a powerful tool of India's diplomacy in this region.[17] India's technical–economic assistance programmes like ITEC, particularly in areas like information technology, are seen as relevant and useful for Central Asia.

The discourses of India's external relations offer insights into the country's strategic culture and the modes of security governance that it fashions. For instance, the propositions of the *Look North Policy* point to secularism, democracy and literacy as national strengths that India and Central Asia share.[18] During the early 1990s, India's foreign policy formulation remained in the rips of conceptual tensions, strategic uncertainty and geopolitical constraints. These diplomatic predicaments reflect India's difficulties in adjusting to the altered realities of the post-Cold War World order.

In this setting, while the discourses of the *Look North Policy* reveal India's aim to attract Central Asia to its sphere of influence, in a Kautilyan fashion, it also resents the regional security governance strategies of other international actors.[19] It focuses on the country-specific strategies targeting individual Central Asian states.[20] The narratives of the *Look North Policy* indicate a desire to encourage regional cooperation between India and the Central Asian states. Pragmatically speaking, the development of strong bilateral relations with the Eurasian States including five Central Asian countries in the region reveals India's attempts to overcome the constraints imposed by its late-comer status in Central Asian affairs, which has further compounded the effects from the lack of a direct physical access to the region.[21] India has adopted an approach aimed at making up for the time lost in respect to its relationship with Central Asian States as compared to other international actors in the region specially in comparison with China.

India's attempt has always been to increase political, cultural and economic ties with the Central Asian Republics (CARs). Central Asia, however, suffers from localized conflicts as well as economic distress. Ethnic tension is continuing in many of these states, making the region susceptible to instability threatening its political and economic development.

Since 1991, India-CARs relations have come a long way. Though numerous political and economic changes have taken place in the recent past in these states but the relationship between India and CARs has gone beyond the historical and cultural ties to a strong political and security cooperation. There are still significant common interests on which India and CAR can accelerate future cooperation. The struggle against terrorism is one major area of cooperation. Both CAR-India shares the view that the problem of drug trafficking and threat of weapons of mass destruction (WMD) are to be addressed jointly. On the situation in Afghanistan both hold similar views. India and the CARs have signed number of agreements to improve their relationship.

Both India and CAR have similar approaches towards major international and regional issues. There have been emergences of new strategic equation and security realignments in the region. Though India is not the key player in the region but these changes provide India both opportunities as well as challenges in the region. After the events of 11 September 2001, India has also started building military technical cooperation with these countries of the region. India is also engaged with CAR's in intelligence sharing,

sharing of joint military experience, and providing training and assistance to Central Asian forces.

Both India and the States of Central Asia have economic complementarities in terms of resources, human resources and markets, which if exploited can broaden cooperation and increase opportunities for joint ventures in banking, insurance, agriculture, IT and pharmaceuticals sector. The Indian pharmaceutical industry has done well in the CARs. Today it accounts for nearly a quarter of the imports into the region.[22] Apart from the Pharmaceutical sector Indian industrialists have also registered an impressive presence in the steel and construction sectors.

India is trying to exploit its expertise in the construction of small and medium-sized hydroelectric plants mainly in Kyrgyzstan and Tajikistan, which have substantial hydropower potential. Also, with Central Asian energy reserves being estimated at 2.7 per cent of world oil reserves (between 13 and 15 billion barrels) and 7 per cent of natural gas reserves (around 270 to 360 trillion cubic feet, mainly in two big fields Kashag and Tangis), the region has potential as a future energy source for India. The main hydrocarbon deposits in the CARs are in Kazakhstan, Turkmenistan and Uzbekistan. India and Uzbekistan signed an agreement to conduct oil and gas exploration in Uzbekistan. Uzbekistan has also agreed to allocate geological territory to Indian companies to explore its hydrocarbon resources. The work is in progress between GAIL (Gas Authority of India Limited) and Uzbekneftogas to build facilities in Uzbekistan to produce LPG (liquefied petroleum gas).[23]

In the field of defence, India had acquired six Ilyushin-78 in-flight refuelling aircrafts from Uzbekistan. Indian aircrafts are being regularly serviced at the Chekalov Aircraft Plant in Tashkent, Uzbekistan, which is indicative of the potential for cooperation between India and Uzbekistan in the aviation sector. Indian experts have been involved in repairing military aircraft in Tajikistan too. Ayni Airbase in Tajikistan happens to be India's first and only foreign military base. Ayni the Air Force Base, is also known as Gissar Air Base, this is basically a military air base in Tajikistan, (10 kms west of the capital of Tajikistan, Dushanbe),[24] which used to be a major military base during the Soviet period.

India's close relationship with Tajikistan helped India to create Ayni airbase there, though it took almost 10 years for India after the disintegration of the Soviet Union to establish this strong connection with Tajikistan. India has spent almost $70 million between 2002 and 2010 to renovate the Ayni base. India has extended the Ayni runway to 3,200 metres and installed state-of-the-art navigational and air defence equipments there. India is very serious about the development of the Ayni air base project to gain a strategic foothold in Central Asia and improve its C3I (Command, Control, Communications and Intelligence) network, to strengthen its operations mainly in Afghanistan. However, this base is still dormant without any fighter jets and Tajik and Indian government both have ruled-out in January 2011, any possibility of deployment of Indian forces at Ayni. [25]The importance of Tajikistan for India cannot be overlooked in any way. Tajikistan's importance in the new great game is likely to unfold in Central and South Asia after the withdrawal of the US led NATO troops from Afghanistan in 2014, which is quite evident in the region.[26] New partners will be formed and it is believed that the regional powers will then be playing major role to establish a stronghold in Afghanistan and in the regional geopolitics. India and Tajikistan wanted to go beyond Ayni airbase, hence, a hospital was constructed with the support of India inside the Tajik area bordering Afghanistan. India is now also looking for bigger security role for itself in Tajikistan.[27]

India and Central Asian State of Turkmenistan are also closely connected with each other. Both the countries share historical and civilizational ties. India had close links with the present-day Turkmenistan since Kushan Empire.[28]The territory of Turkmenistan was located at the crossroads of seven caravan routes and it became an important trade link between India, Central Asia and Europe from the very early times. India and Turkmenistan share close political understanding between each other on key regional and international issues.

Although Turkmenistan is a young state, its ties with India date back to Harappa and Indus Valley civilization and the Bronze Age settlements in the South and Western region of Turkmenistan such as Merv, Nisa and Dehistan. In the southern capital of Merv there are eight main Gates which are called as the Indian Gates and are still preserved along with the remnants of several caravan-serais for Indian traders. Both the Countries were connected through the Silk Route (i.e. the road from the Karakoram Mountains on the way towards the Khunjerab Pass or across the Hindu Kush mountains on the route towards Khyber Pass)[29] and the relationship became close during the Silk Route trading days.

During the period of XIII-XVI centuries Muhammed Bayram Khan, the mentor of Akbar Shah and Chief Commander of (India's) Mughal Army was a Turkmen, who belonged to Baharlu Qara Qoyunlu Turkmens, also called as the Black Sheep of Turkomans, who ruled the territory of Azerbaijan, Armenia and Iraq during 14-15 centuries. Mirza Abdur Rahim Khan-i-Khanan, the famous poet and the philosopher became one of Akbar's nine prominent ministers in the *Navaratnas* (one out of nine). Another great son of Baharlu Qara Qoyunlu was Turkmen Sultan Quliul-Mulk, who migrated to Deccan and served under Mohammad Shah Bahmani Sultan, in middle of XVI century. Later he conquered Golconda (presently in South of India) and established the Qutb Shahi dynasty in India. All eight kings of this dynasty, who ruled in Golkonda during the 171 years, were great academics.[30]They not only patronized the economy and architecture in Hyderabad (now south Indian city), but also contributed for the development of Persian culture, local languages and science.

In the 17th century Mughal Prince Shah Jahan built in New Delhi 14 gates, one of which was named in the honor of the Turkmen, who played a key role in the Delhi Sultanate and Mughal Empire. In Aligarh, (one of the northern cities of India) the second Turkmen Gate was built and the nearby town is still called as Turkmen town. On the way towards the city of Aligarh one can still find a place of Bairam Khan and a well-known village of Khan-Khana which is named after Abdurahim Khan-i-Khanan.[31]All these factors underline the age-old linkages between India and Turkmenistan.

The new period of contacts between the two sides were revived after India gained its independence on August 15, 1947. India's first Prime Minister Jawaharlal Nehru accompanied by Indira Gandhi visited Ashgabat on June 14, 1955.[32]Since their visit to Turkmenistan, hundreds of girls have been named after Indira Gandhi. Many streets, clubs and cultural centers even today are named after J.L. Nehru and Indira. In Ashgabat, a leading Medical College has been named after Indira Gandhi. Bollywood film actor Raj Kapoor and his films are very popular till date in Turkmenistan.

Diplomatic relationship between the two countries was established on 20th April 1992. India opened its Embassy in Ashgabat on January 1994.[33] One year later the diplomatic mission of Turkmenistan was established in New Delhi. From time to time, various high level Ministerial visits have been regularly taking place between the two countries.

India-Turkmenistan energy cooperation is moving smoothly particularly in the implementation of the TAPI project. TAPI is expected to meet the growing energy needs of South Asia. TAPI gas pipeline project has been described by the participant countries as the 'Pipeline of Peace' and a 'Reflection of Desire'. [34]The implementation of TAPI project will bring Central Asia and South Asia much closer in enduring energy project, integrating regional countries for development and prosperity. TAPI can support by providing natural gas for fulfilling the economic development plans and for implementing clean energy program.[35] TAPI can become a best example of growing regional integration process.

The Dovletabad deposits, which contain 4.5 to 16 thousand cubic meters (tcm) of gas, can supply with the necessary volumes of gas. Currently, experts estimate Turkmenistan's total geological reserves as 71.21 billion tons of equivalent fuel, of which 53.01 billion tons are land reserves and 18.2 billion tons are offshore reserves. Turkmen government source report mentioned that, the proven gas reserves are estimated at 25.213 trillion of cubic meters.[36] Turkmenistan's energy potential has been estimated lately as 45.44 billion tons of equivalent fuel.

The TAPI pipeline starting from Turkmenistan's Dauletabad gas fields passing through Herat and Kandahar will follow Afghanistan's Ring Road. Further, the pipeline would extend to the cities of Quetta and Multan in Pakistan and connect to the Indian city of Fazilka at the Indo-Pak border. The 1800 km. pipeline can carry 90 million standard cubic meters of gas a day for 30 years period. India and Pakistan is expected to get 38mmscmd each. The $7.6 billion, TAPI pipeline first supplies are planned for 2019.[37] TAPI pipeline offers benefits to all four participating countries and has the potential to bring regional countries closer to each other improving the connectivity and linkages.

TAPI will provide alternative for exporting energy resources to other countries too. TAPI is expected to move beyond traditional adversaries between the neighbouring countries, as this project addresses and emphasises on the economic development and energy security concerns above geopolitics.[38] This pipeline project with the governmental support from all the four participating countries along with the external support by the regional development agencies is considered as beneficial for all the participants say it consumer, supplier and also the financers.

TAPI pipeline is also expected to provide new business opportunities for the gas and engineering industries. ADB (Asian development Bank) is leading stakeholder of the project. Oil and gas firms such as Chevron, Exxon, Gazprom are also part of the project apart from National Oil Companies (NOC) of the participant countries. All the participant countries involved their NOC's in this project for example Gas Authority of India, Interstate Gas System from Pakistan; Afghan Gas Enterprise from Afghanistan and Turkmen-Gaz from Turkmenistan formed a joint venture named TAPI Pipeline Company Limited for working together in this project.[39] Though, current security issues related to Afghanistan & Pakistan is of concern, economic issues for financing the pipeline full of risk was also of concern and reason for this delay. But the intensified contacts for addressing security issues established among the four participants of this project, indicates growing partnership and support for TAPI.

Physical connectivity and access to energy resources is one of the important elements of the India-Turkmen bilateral partnership and TAPI is a key project in this sphere. At present, the debate on TAPI indicates that TAPI will be successful provided all the stakeholders work together to ensure that negative forces hostile to the success of this project be taken care in an appropriate manner, as any violence or disruption can threaten prosperity of the region that is expected to come through TAPI. Support of local government and cooperation of all the partners are important to address the security challenges as well as ensure technical and commercial viability of the project to make energy available at the low cost to the larger sections of the regional population.

The discourse among the policy makers in India on TAPI is that this will enhance India's 'Connect Central Asia', policy and will also boost new regionalism reviving the ancient *Silk Route* connectivity. India presently does not have inter-country gas pipelines and relies only on domestic sources of gas and imported LNG supply. India's gas demand is projected to grow to 746 mmscmd by 2029–2030 and in the face of declining production from the KG D6 gas fields, India needs to find alternate and cheap sources of natural gas to fulfill its ambitious economic development and clean energy agenda and TAPI is expected to fulfill this requirement.[40] During last (22nd) steering committee meeting of TAPI held at Ashgabat on 6th - 8th of August 2015, it was decided that with a 51% shareholding, Turkmen-Gaz would be the consortium leader and the other national oil companies would hold equal shares of the remaining 49%.[41] Now TAPI project seems to be moving in the right direction. TAPI's success is win-win for all the participant countries, hence, it is expected that the attitude of all the four partners will be to complete this project as fast as possible and make this as a politically and economically viable mission. TAPI dream project is now becoming reality with the political will, positive diplomatic decision and close cooperation among participating countries. At present, both countries are providing each other mutual support in the international arena, expanding multilateral cooperation in the framework of the international structures. Turkmenistan has supported India's candidature for a permanent seat in the Security Council of the United Nation. India highly value the support extended by Turkmenistan for India's candidature.

During the early years of Independence of Turkmenistan, India provided the necessary financial and other assistance to the Government of Turkmenistan. Joint venture between Turkmenistan and Indian pharmaceutical company Turkmenderman-Ajanta Pharma Ltd has been functioning very well in Ashgabat since its establishment in December 1998, (it has an ultra-modern plant and manufactures 70 different types of medicines).[42]Other joint ventures between both the Nations are also going on well like in the areas of juice making, food and wool processing sectors. In July 2009, a mutual agreement was signed by the Chamber of Commerce and Industry of Turkmenistan and the India-CIS Chamber of Commerce and Industry. There was a steady growth of trade between two countries[43] Joint ventures between Indian and Turkmenistan's construction companies are taking place for past few years and are becoming partners in infrastructural development projects.

There is huge scope for further enhancing multi-faceted cooperation between India and Turkmenistan from economy and trade to culture, science, technology and education. Two countries have already established mechanisms for boosting cooperation in various fields. India-Turkmenistan Inter-Governmental Commission (IGC) on Trade, Economic, Scientific and Technological Cooperation has been meeting regularly every year. Simultaneously a Joint Working Group on Energy was also set up to facilitate for smooth energy cooperation. The Turkmenisatn-Indian Industrial Training Centre has been functioning in Ashgabat since December 2002. Machine tools worth over half a million US dollars have been gifted to the Centre by the Government of India under ITEC program. More than 250 Turkmenistan citizens have availed training facilities under this program. Turkmenistan Airlines runs two flights every week between Delhi and Ashgabat and weekly nine flights between Amritsar and Ashgabat. Turkmen students avails the opportunity to study in Indian Universities under the ICCR (Indian Council for Cultural Research) cultural exchange programme and since 2009, a Hindi Chair is functioning in the Turkmenistan National Institute of World Languages in Ashgabat. Experts and scientists from various scientific centers of Turkmenistan are regularly visiting India to gather research materials for manuscripts on the bilateral relations and to know more about the history of India-Turkmenistan relations.[44]All these focus on the deep relationship between both the States and also ensure that this relationship will flourish in the coming years.

India-Kazakhstan cooperation is also going on smoothly for many years now. India was one of the first countries to establish diplomatic relationship with Kazakhstan. Strategic Partnership agreement between India and Kazakhstan was signed during

President of Kazakhstan Nursultan Nazerbaiev's official visit to India in the year 2009, signing of strategic partnership increase comprehensive cooperation in all spheres, including political, economic, science and technology, military and technical cooperation in counter-terrorism mechanism, education and human resources development. India and Kazakhstan also signed number of Agreements and MoUs in the areas of oil and gas, in nuclear energy sector and on space sector. Kazakhstan is also the largest trade partner of India in Central Asia today. Both India and Kazakhstan understand the need for using their vast experience, international exposure and synergy is to work jointly. In the energy cooperation, besides downstream projects, Indian companies are working in petrochemical sphere in Kazakhstan. ONGC, IOC and GAIL (India) planning to set-up Gas Based Petrochemical Plant in Kazakhstan. Similarly, NTPC of India is looking to establish a coal based power station and possibility for renovating the existing power plants in Kazakhstan. The NTPC is also thinking of importing coal from Kazakhstan to meet its existing needs in power generation in India.[45]

India and Kazakhstan is also working on cooperation in health and medical sector. The Joint Committee on S&T is now working jointly on biotechnology, nanotechnology, solar energy and catalyses as the priority areas. To facilitate more student and teacher exchanges, an agreement on cooperation in the field of education is under consideration. Many specialists, experts and scholars from Kazakhstan attend ITEC (Indian Technical & Economic Cooperation Programme) courses every year.[46]At present, exchange in the area of tourism is going on smoothly. It has become a good tradition to hold the Kazakhstan-India Travel and Tourism Fair in New Delhi on an annual basis.

Kazakhstan and India are reliable partners not only on the bilateral level, but also within international organizations. Kazakhstan supports India's candidacy for UNSC (United

Nations Security Council) permanent membership. India has also supported Kazakhstan's aspiration to become the WTO member.[47]Kazakhstan was one of the strong supporters of India at NSG meeting in Vienna. India and Kazakhstan are also working together within SCO, especially within Regional Counter Terrorist Structure (RCTS). The visit by the President of Kazakhstan Nur-Sultan Nazarbayev as the Chief Guest for India's Republic Day celebration symbolizes the importance attached by Government of India to Kazakhstan and it is expected that the relationship will thrive in the coming years too.

Since the independence of Kyrgyzstan on 31st August, 1991, India was among the first to establish diplomatic relations in 1992. The resident Mission of India was set up in Kyrgyzstan in the year 1994.[48]Political ties with the Kyrgyz Republic have been traditionally warm and friendly. The Kyrgyz leadership have been largely supportive of India's stand on Kashmir and have welcomed the ongoing peace process. Kyrgyzstan also supports India's bid for permanent seat at UNSC and India's role in the Shanghai Cooperation Organization (SCO).

Both countries share common concerns on threat of terrorism, extremism and drug–trafficking. Since the establishment of diplomatic relations in 1992, the two countries have signed several framework agreements on culture, trade and economic cooperation, civil aviation, investment promotion and protection, avoidance of double taxation, consular convention etc. At the institutional level, foreign office consultations have provided a useful forum for exchange of views on bilateral and international issues, the two countries signed agreement for co-operation and investments in mineral exploration and development, in the food processing sector, in chemical and petrochemical sector, in the information technology sector, in healthcare sector, in science & technology, in tourism, in education, in sports & culture.

Technical assistance under the Indian Technical and Economic Cooperation (ITEC) Program, particularly in terms of human resources development, is the cornerstone of India's economic involvement in Kyrgyzstan. Kyrgyzstan has been allotted 60 slots on an annual basis for civilian training under ITEC.[49]Since 1992, more than 700 professionals from Kyrgyzstan have received training in India.

India and Central Asian States want to be part of an extended trade network through the North–South transport corridor too. India and Central Asian States are closely working with each other on the security sectors too as the three CAR States bordering Afghanistan i.e. Uzbekistan, Tajikistan and Turkmenistan can curb security threats emanating from Afghanistan. There has been an articulated policy of India to integrate Central Asia with India and consider an observer status for the CARs in SAARC forum. India's membership in the Economic Cooperation Organization (ECO) can also strengthen India's economic relationship with the CARs and could lead the relationship further creating a meaningful partnership. There is also a need to look for ways to increase people-to-people contacts and step-up information sharing

The overall outlook on the region suggests that for India, there is an enormous scope and potential to engage in meaningful and fruitful politico-economic cooperation with the CARs. India and CAR both got immense potential to offer each other but there is a need to place these realizations on the fast track.

India-South Caucasus Relationship

Friendly relationships between India and South Caucasus have existed for more than four thousand years. Affinities of culture, language and mythology brought these two regions closer. The Caucasus region is known as a crossroads, a meeting point of different people, different cultures and different political, social, and economic forces where the flow of people and products from the various places passed through for many years. The region is the site of the convergence and sometimes the collision of political and economic ideas that has been their origins in four different centuries i.e. in the eighteenth, in the nineteenth, and even in the twenty-first century.[50] However, today, there is a problem within these South Caucasus Countries as two of them are the traditional rivals and the differences and conflict within these two nations are continuing even today. Like Azeris and Armenians have been at war for over a decade, and the Georgians and the Abkhaz have been clashing with each-other since independence and having continuous problems with Russia. Though all these three states could benefit from standing together, however, it is a difficult task for new states to maximize their foreign policy potential. The South Caucasus States are also uncomfortable placing too much reliance on their immediate neighbours and are less likely to develop strong cooperative institutions.

In the South Caucasus State of Armenia from 149 B.C. till A.D. 301 there existed a Hindu colony. As far back as the fifth century Armenian traders regularly traded in Indian muslin, spices, precious stones and herbs. Many Armenians who became citizens of India were traders, government servants and academics. Some Armenians were even involved in India's independence movement and even served in the Indian Army. Armenians were mostly residents of Chennai, Mumbai, Kolkata and Surat but currently there are hardly hundred Armenians in India and mostly living in Kolkata. The first Armenian Constitution was written in Chennai.[51] Today, the main concern of the Armenian Church Committee of Kolkata is to preserve the Armenian heritage and properties such as the Armenian College and Philanthropic Academy. India and Armenia are both keen to cooperate with each other in politico-security and economic spheres and grow the relationship further.

India-Azerbaijan relations started since the 10th century when the famous Silk Route connected India with the Central Eurasian region. Azerbaijan declared its independence on October 18, 1991. Earlier, it was a part of the former Soviet Union. India recognized Azerbaijan in December 1991 and established diplomatic relations on February 28, 1992.[52] The friendship between the people of Azerbaijan and India has continued for hundreds of years now. Azerbaijan was connected with India through Silk Route. This has maintained India's relations with the whole region. The Silk Route passed through the Caspian region, before twisting towards the Mediterranean coastline. The route approached the eastern Caspian Sea after spanning Uzboy River which is now part of the state of Turkmenistan in Central Asia.

The Silk Route connecting the territory of Azerbaijan passed on to the western side of the Caspian Sea where the two similar roads emerged. One of them moved towards the west along the Kur River till it reached the Georgian Black Sea coast. Another route moved towards the north along the western Caspian coastline and entered Caucasia through the gates of Derbent and finally ended at the Greek city near the Black Sea.

Owing to Azerbaijan's central location, it became the hub for merchants travelling from India towards Europe. Consequently, Baku, the capital of Azerbaijan, emerged as the largest trade centre on the long stretch of the Silk Route. Trade was carried between the two countries over the Silk Route. The links were cemented and strengthened when master craftsmen from Tabriz, (principal city of Iranian Azerbaijan) got involved in the construction of the famous historical monument of India, the Taj Mahal, in the city of Agra.[53]

Another significant landmark that connected India with Azerbaijan is the Ateshgah Monument near Baku, a surviving proof of the ancient relationship between India and Azerbaijan. The temple of Ateshgah, 15 kms from the Azeri capital Baku, is one of the significant reminders of India's close ties with the region spanning across the Caspian Sea. In the middle ages, the Hindu traders mostly from Multan and Sindh visited Azerbaijan for the Silk Road trade. The Atashgah temple in Surakhani was used by the traders for worshipping while they rested in that area.[54] While they were there, they used to practice religious ceremonies. According to historical sources, the local people also worshipped at Atashgah temple because of the famous seven holes with burning flames. Thus, the name Surakhani which means holes with burning fires became famous. Inside the temple a cubicle brick structure is built around a fire which was first fuelled by natural gas seeping out of the ground. Flames leaped out of four chimneys raised on top of this structure. Every evening, these fires cast a deep orange glow over the enclosure. An inscription in Sanskrit and Gurmukhi above the narrow arched entrance of this monument is a prominent affirmation of Azerbaijan's historical ties with India.[55]

The Ateshgah monument, also called the 'fire worshipper's temple', traces its origins to Zoroastrianism, which took root in ancient Azerbaijan as this land is the mother of Zoroastrianism. Between the late 17th and mid-19th century, Indian traders built this complex with number of guest rooms, stables and prayer rooms. This temple has also been compared with the Sri Jwalaji temple of fire in India. Though Azerbaijan is a Muslim country, even then there are few Azeri people who have become followers of 'Hare Krishna' too, represented by members of ISKCON.[56] India and Azerbaijan have developed economic ties with each other but there are still several areas of cooperation that need to be explored. There are huge opportunities for mutual investments. However, there is a need to create a friendly and conducive atmosphere for mutual trade and enhancing friendly relations between business communities of the two nations.

The two sides are looking at opportunities for cooperating in the field of petro - chemical industry, especially in the petroleum refining sector. They are also seeking to enhance technical cooperation and find possibilities for exchange of views in the field of agriculture. Today, much of the trade of Indian items with Azerbaijan is carried out through UAE, which does not get reflected in the trade statistics. Many Indian pharmaceutical companies are successfully competing with European companies in the markets of Azerbaijan. Bharat Heavy Electricals Limited (BHEL) has executed a project for Az-Energy, for the supply and installation of power generators for the Mingechevir Power Plant in Azerbaijan.[57] Gujarat has supplied bauxite (aluminum ore) and aluminum concentrate to the aluminum plants in Ganja and Sumgait, these two Azeri Cities, have contributed largely to increase India's exports to Azerbaijan.

During the Soviet period, the educational institutions in Azerbaijan were a favourite destination for Indian students. However, at present there are around 500 Indian students in Azerbaijan mainly for medical and technical studies. Indians make their presence felt in various sectors in Azerbaijan even today. A few former Indian students have settled there and are now engaged in trading, running hospitality businesses and dealing in pharmaceuticals. The pharmaceutical sector is well represented by Indian nationals in Azerbaijan and some of them even established their representative offices there. If the oil and gas industry in Azerbaijan takes off as a global energy supplier in the near future, this development can be of immense benefit for India. India has shown interest for entering into a long-term contract with Azerbaijan for the supply of crude oil.

The traditional folklore 'Laila-Majnu', on which several Hindi Bollywood movies have been made, can be traced to Azerbaijan. The great Azerbaijani poet, Nizami Ganjavi, who lived in the 12th century, established a new trend in poetry-the epic-romantic genre and wrote 'Laila–Majnu'. Even today Laila-Majnu, Shireen-Farhad and other romantic folklores traced to Azerbaijan remain popular in India. Bollywood superstars are still famous in Azerbaijan among the younger as well as older generations. Till date, Bollywood's legendary actors Raj Kapoor and Nargis, are still favourites in Azerbaijan.

The historic linkages are also noted by Azerbaijani-origins of Babur, the founder of the Mughal dynasty in India. The architect of the outstanding monuments constructed during the Mughal period, including Humayun's tomb in Delhi, was from Azerbaijan. Architect Agha Mirek Ghiyas was the principal architect of Humayun's Tomb in New Delhi and Physician Rugn addin Masud Masihi was a personal physician of Jahangir from 1576-1655. He did medical practices mainly in the Indian cities of Agra, Allahabad and Jaipur.[58] All these indicate that cultural affinity between people of the two countries is still very strong. Another very significant cultural linkage is that the most popular names used in Azerbaijan are Indian names, including that of the late Prime Minister Indira Gandhi and film star Nargis. One can find quite a few Indiras and Nargises in Azerbaijan. Both the countries can renew the old relations in the same magnitude as during the silk route days, benefiting both societies in every possible manner. By sharing information and by developing people to people contact and awareness in both nations about one another, it is possible to strengthen the mutually beneficial relationship.

Bilateral relationship between India and Georgia also goes back to several centuries. Georgia has consistently supported India's position on Jammu and Kashmir and India's candidature to the UN Security Council. Both sides have emphasized the need to combat international terrorism and separatism. Georgia also supports India's draft Comprehensive Convention on International Terrorism (CCIT). Georgia's unstable political situation has slowed down the growth in trade and economic cooperation between the two countries. India's main exports to Georgia are pharmaceuticals and consumer durables. Import comprises of metals like aluminium, copper and ferrous. Indian construction company the Punj Lloyd, was a major sub-contractor for the construction of Georgian part of the Baku-Tbilisi-Ceyhan (BTC) oil pipeline. Georgian and Indian relations have much longer history consisting of more than thousand years.

There are many literature and folk evidences mention that Georgia and India already have links with each other for centuries. The twelfth century Georgian epic poet Shota Rustaveli wrote a poem "Knight in the Panther's Skin" and the main character the brave prince is Indian. Georgian traveler of the 18th and 19th centuries Rafiel Danibegashvili who travelled to India several times, wrote a book called "Travel to India of the Merchant Rafiel Danibegashvili," which is also translated into many languages including Hindi.

Many Georgian poets have been influenced by the Nobel laureate Rabindranath Tagore. His famous "Gitanjali", has been translated into Georgian language almost 50 years ago, by famous Georgian poet Tamaz Chkhenkeli. In the 20th century, Pandit Jawaharlal Nehru, Indira Gandhi and former Indian Prime Minister Atal Bihari Vajpayee have travelled to Georgia while Georgia was under Soviet Union. India was one of the first countries in the World to recognize Georgia's independence in UN in 1992. Since 1992, India and Georgia have established diplomatic relationship.

After the establishment of the Embassy of Georgia in New Delhi, the relationship became more comprehensive and the level of awareness about Georgia increased. Many new projects between two Nations started and many of them are under process. The most significant projects that are of the highest importance are the Baku-Tbilisi-Jeihan and Baku-Tbilisi-Erzerum gas pipelines which are already operational. In its turn BTE gas pipeline has an option to be connected to the future Nabucco Pipeline which is expected to transport natural gas from Caspian Countries to other Countries of Europe.[59] In current political and economic situation countries participating in this project proved to be the most reliable suppliers of oil and gas from the Caspian Sea to the European Markets. It is also expected that BTC pipeline will be connected with TAPI pipeline and possibility of gas flow through this pipeline to India will be made possible in near future. Besides natural resources, this region is also considered as a trade hub for Asian and European producers. Georgian ports and free trade zones on the Black Sea, well maintained railway and highway system provide to regional producers the best options for import and export of goods. Both India and Georgia have signed several important bilateral agreements and many more are under process, which will make the bi-lateral cooperation further intense.

Conclusion

India and the Eurasian states of Russia, Central Asia and South Caucasus have come a long way over the period of time and developed close cooperation in number of spheres. However, there are still many glaring weaknesses in India's policy and approach towards the region. Unfortunately, in the early years after the independence of these States, India was unable to optimally convert the traditional goodwill into contemporary influence. Even at the governmental level, India paid inadequate attention to these States initially. While resident Embassies were opened in all these countries, infrequent high-level visits conveyed the impression to these countries that India was not looking at this region as seriously as were by other major global/regional powers. Nor have India's businessmen, industrialists and bankers shown great interest in these countries during early 1990's. There is a reason for this as the emergence of these newly independent States coincided with India's own economic liberalization, when the focus of India was towards developed countries from where India hoped to get investments and technological support, which was crucial during the same time and these countries were also under transition and were also moving towards West.

In the beginning of 1990's, when these Eurasian states became independent; many Indian companies had to bear severe loses. Even, today many major Indian companies are skeptical to start investment or start business project with the States of Caucasus and Central Asia, due to poor air connectivity, visa problems, high corruption rate, lack of proper banking facilities etc. all these reasons have contributed to in-adequate trade and economic cooperation. All the major global players, including United States, European Countries, as well as, China have a strong presence in the region and energy has emerged as an additional factor in strategic equations. India's economic relations have woefully lagged behind the political relationship, principally because India was not economically rich enough in the early 1990's to provide financial support to these newly independent Eurasian States of former Soviet Union nor is its business, industrial and financial community sufficiently motivated or has been aggressive enough to be able to overcome the problems in dealing with the countries of this region in the early and mid of 1990's. For India to protect and preserve its interests in the region need to have close consultation and cooperation with other major powers having interest and a presence in the region. This could be done within the ongoing Russia-India-China (RIC) trilateral framework. It can also be considered within the framework of the SCO and play significant role on an equal footing with the other major players like the US, European Countries, Japan, Russia and China.

India and all the countries of Eurasia i.e. Russia, Central Asia and Caucasus are determined to strengthen the ties matching with the historical ties in the contemporary era. However, there is a need to review and re-energise its efforts to manage the new set of challenges, to ensure the security and to improve the connectivity with each other. There is tremendous scope for improving bilateral relationship for satisfying the countries immediate as well as the long term needs. From the point of view to build a stable, prosperous and peaceful region, it is important to increase dialogue with each other in the region and establish people to people contact. Hence, these countries along with India need to participate in the development of the region together for establishing mutually beneficial partnership and cooperation to set the movement of growth and prosperity.

Endnotes

1 Nandkumar T., "Celebrating 60 years of Indo-Russian ties", *Hindu*, Jun 12, 2007.

2 India-Russia Relations in http://www.axisglobe.com/article.asp?article7=52.

3 A. Mantysky, "Russian-Indian Strategic Partnership on a New Anvil", in P.L. Das and Andrei M. Nazarkin (eds.), *India and Russia Strategic Synergy Emerging*, Delhi: Author Press, 2007, pp. 15–20.

4 V.D. Chopra, "Indo-Russian Defence Cooperation and India's Independence and Sovereignty". in V.D. Chopra (ed.), *New Trends in Indo-Russian Relations*, Delhi: Kalpaz, 2003, pp. 121–22.

5 Anuradha Chenoy, "A Defining Moment", *Frontline*, 17(21), 14-27 October 2000.

6 Sergei Lavrov, "Russia and India: Mutually Beneficial Cooperation and Strategic Partnership", *International Affairs*, Vol.53, No.3, 2007, pp24-29.

7 Report from Eurasian Division, MEA.

8 Rajat Pandit, "Russia to Remain Top Arms Supplier to India", *Times of India*, New Delhi, Jan. 22, 2007.

9 "India, China, Russia Foreign Ministers to Hold Talks in Feb.", *Times of India*, 29 January 2007.

10 "India-Central Asia Economic Relations", A Report of RIS/CII Seminar RIS-DP # 94/2005, May 2005.

11 Sandeep Unnithan, "Cruise Control", *India Today*, 2 May, 2005.

12 Oksana Antonenko, *The EU Should not Ignore the Shanghai Co-operation Organisation*, Policy Brief, Centre for European Studies, London, May 2009.

13 Prasanna Patsani, 'Indo-Russian Togetherness in the New Millennium' in Prasanna Patsani, Ed., *India-Russia, Towards Strategic Partnership*, Samskriti, New Delhi, 2002,pp.179-185.

14 Anita Singh, "India's Relations with Russia and Central Asia", *International Affairs*, 71(1), January 1999, pp. 69-81.

15 Richard Pomfret, "The Economic Cooperation Organization: Current Status and Future Prospects", *Europe-Asia Studies*, 49(4), July 1997, pp. 649–59.

16 M.S. Roy, "India's Interest in Central Asia", *Strategic Analysis*, Vol.34, (12), March 2001, pp. 2273–89.

17 Lena Jonson, *Vladimir Putin and Central Asia*, London: I.B. Taurus, 2004, pp. 103–12.

18 See"India-Central Asia Economic Relations", A Report of RIS/CII Seminar RIS-DP # 94/2005, May 2005.

19 Firdous T., "India and Central Asia", in M.A.Kaw and A.A. Banday (eds.) *Central Asia Introspection*, Crown Press, Srinagar, 2006,pp.321-322.

20 See Anita Singh, "India's Relations with Russia and Central Asia", *International Affairs*, 71(1), January 1995, pp. 69.

21 See Faultline of Conflict in Central Asia and the South Caucasus, RAND Document, RAND Publications, 2003. Also see Kavalski, 2007, p. 854.

22 Jyotsna Bakshi, *Russia and India: From Ideology to Geopolitics*, Delhi: Dev Publication, 1999, pp. 207–18.

23 Firdous T., "India and Central Asia", in M.A.Kaw and A.A. Banday eds. *Central Asia Introspection*, Crown Press, Srinagar, 2006,pp.321-322.

24 M. Dhar, "Indo-Russian Relations are Re-Energising", *New Theme*, VII(2), April 2007, pp 26–7.

25 Report from Tajikistan Embassy in New Delhi 2013.

26 "India looking for energy supplies in Central Asia", 13 September 2006, available at http://www.asianews.it/index.php?art=7200&l=en.

27 Tabata Shinichiro (ed.), *Dependent on Oil and Gas: Russia's Integration in to the World Economy*, Japan: Osamu Ieda, 2006, pp. 1-7.

28 Lalit Manshigh, India-Russia Enduring Ties, pp. 28-29 and Nirmala Joshi, "Evolution of Indo-Russian Relations, pp.37-29, in *India and Russia : 60 Years of fruitful Relationship*, Delhi: Unity International, Jan.2009.

29 S. Blank, "India: The New Central Asian Player", available at www. eurasianet.org/departments/insight/articles/eav062606a.shtml.

30 Flex Yurlov, "Russia and India: Partners in World Politics". In Das and Nazarkin eds., *India and Russia: Strategic Synergy Emerging*, pp. 61–74. 2007.

31 R.G. Gidadhubli, "India's Economic Relations with Russia: Performance and Potentialities", in Das and Nazarkin (eds.) n. 5.

32 Olga Lukash, Policy Brief on *India-Ukraine Bi-lateral Relations*, Institute for World Economics, Kiev, 2007.

33 Turkmen Government Report.

34 "TAPI will meet Pakistan, India energy concerns", *The Statesman*, 15th December 2015.

35 "TAPI Project likely get start", *Deccan Herald*, available at http://www.deccanherald.com/content/515890/tapi-project-likely-kick-start.html, accessed on 12th December 2015.

36 Firdous T., "India and Central Asia", in M.A.Kaw and A.A. Banday eds. *Central Asia Introspection*, Crown Press, Srinagar, 2006, pp.321-322.

37 "India-Central Asia Economic Relations", Report of RIS/CII Seminar RIS-DP # 94/2005, May 2005.

38 Narula Kapil, "TAPI Pipeline Inching from Dream to Reality", available at https://www.indrastra.com/2015/12/FEATURED-TAPI-Pipeline-Inching-from-Dreams-to-Reality-by-Kapil-Narula-0513. html, accessed on 10th December 2015.

39 Ministry of External Affairs Report August 2015.

40 "Regional-Economic-Cooperation-Creates-the-TAPI-Pipeline"., available at http://www.economywatch.com/features/ Regional-Economic-Cooperation-Creates-the-TAPI-Pipeline1204.html, accessed on 10th December 2015.

41 Turkmen Foreign Ministry Report, August 2015.

42 Turkmen Embassy Report.

43 Turkmen Foreign Minsitry Report.

44 Ministry of External Affairs Report.

45 Santhanam K, Baizakova K, Dwivedi R eds. *India-Kazakhstan Perspective*, Anamaya Publishers, 2007.

46 Santhanam K. Sultanov Bulat eds. *India-Kazakhstan relations : Enhancing the Partnership* Anamaya Publishers, 2006.

47 Kazakh Embassy Report.

48 Santhanam K, Dwivedi R. eds *India-Kyrgyz Relations: Perspective and Prospects*, Anamaya Publishers 2006.

49 Kazakhstan Country analysis Brief, EIA, 2008.

50 Kundu Das Nivedita, *Russia and its Near Abroad: Strategic Dynamics and Implications*, Authors Press, Delhi, 2008.

51 ibid.

52 Kundu Das Nivedita Ed. *India-Azerbaijan: the Silk Route Connections*, Academic Foundation, New Delhi 2012.

53 Ibid.

54 Azerbaijan, Report of Embassy of India, available at http://meaindia. nic.in/foreignrelation/azerbaijan.htm, 2007.

55 Information collected during authors visit to Atsgha Temple in Baku, Azerbaijan during August 2014.

56 Sadiqoglu Afet, Azerbaijan-Hindustan Relations, Nurlan, Baku, 2009, pp5-8.

57 Svante E. Cornell, "Security Threats and Challenges in Caucasus after 9/11", in Ariel Cohen ed, Eursaia in Balance: The US and the Regional Power Shift, Aldershot: Ashgate Publishing Ltd, 2005, pp.44.

58 Ibid.

59 Ibid.

References

Central Asia Regional Overview, UNHCR Global Report 2000, available at http://www.unhcr.org/cgibin/texis/vtx/home/opendocPDFViewer. html?docid=3e23eb617&query=afghans.

Alexander Zelitchenko, "Central Asia at Risk From Post-2014 Afghanistan", available at https://iwpr.net/global-voices/central-asia-risk-from-post-2014-afghanistan

LailumaNoori(2015), "Extremist movements in north a threat to Central Asia, experts", The Kabul Times, October 11, available at http://thekabultimes.gov.af/index.php/opinions/politics/8335-extremist-movements-in-north-a-threat-to-central-asia-experts.html.

Mathieu Guidère (2012), "Historical Dictionary of Islamic Fundamentalism", Maryland: Scarecrow Press Inc.

S. Frederick Starr (2005), "A 'Greater Central Asia Partnership' for Afghanistan and Its Neighbors", Silk Road Paper, available at http://www.silkroadstudies.org/resources/pdf/SilkRoadPapers/2005_starr_a-greater-central-asia-partnership.pdf.

NargisKassenova (2014), "Relations between Afghanistan and Central Asian states after 2014: Incentives, Constraints and Prospects", SIPRI, available at http://books.sipri.org/files/misc/SIPRI14wcaNK.pdf.

Horton S. "How Central is Central Asia?", Part 3/3, You Tube, available at https://www.youtube.com/watch?v=9D_ZjHHi1vo, October 29, 2010,

Cooley A., "Great Games, Local Rules: The New Power Contest in Central Asia", Oxford University Press, 2012, pp.120-122

Rahimov, Mirzohid and Galina Urazaeva. *Central Asian Nations and Border Issues,* Conflict Studies Research Centre Report, Central Asian Series, 05/10, March 2005.

Phillips, Andrew and Paul James. "National Identity Between Tradition and Reflexive Modernisation: The Contradictions of Central Asia", *National Identities,* vol.3, no.1, 2001.

Rahimov, Mirzohid. "From Soviet Republics to Independent Countries: Challenges of Transition in Central Asia", *Perspectives on Global Development and Technology,* vol.6, issues.1-3, 2007.

Simonsen, Sven Gunnar. "Between Minority Rights and Civil Liberties: Russia's Discourse over 'Nationality' Registration and the Internal Passport", *Nationalities Papers,* vol. 33, no. 2, June 2005.

Saray, Mehmet. "The Russian Conquest of Central Asia", *Central Asian Survey,* vol.2, no.3, 1982.

India's Emerging Partnership in Eurasia

Stephen Aris, "Managing Central Asia: Russia's Approach", Swiss Federal University of Zurich, at http://www.isn.ethz.ch/isn/Digital-Library/Articles/Special-Feature/Detail/?lng=en&id=160464&contextid774=160464&contextid775=160462&tabid=1454180197, March 2013

Gulshan Sachdeva, India's Objectives in Central Asia, School of International Studies, Jawaharlal Nehru University, at http://uschinacenter.as.nyu.edu/docs/IO/23889/Sachdeva_Abs.pdf

Roman Muzalevsky, "India's 'Connect Central Asia' Policy Seeks to Compensate for Lost Time", "Eurasia Daily Monitor", Volume: 9 Issue: 176, available at http://www.jamestown.org/single/?no_cache=1&tx_ttnews%5Btt_news%5D=39891

"Regional-Economic-Cooperation-Creates-the-TAPI-Pipeline"., available at http://www.economywatch.com/features/Regional-Economic-Cooperation-Creates-the-TAPI-Pipeline1204.html

~ 48 ~

2

Silk Route Connectivity and the Regional Transport Corridors

Silk Route, one of the greatest sagas of human endeavour is being revived in the view of the fast changing world order, however, with varying perceptions. The idea of reviving the *Silk Route* connectivity and bringing the countries of the Eurasian region with the neighbouring states is a mega cross-border project with number of challenges ahead. However these challenges could be accomplished with close regional cooperation, strong political will and economic support. Many countries in the region are already involved in the process of reviving the *Silk Route*.[1]

Since 1990, the revival of the '*Silk Route*' was being discussed enthusiastically at all levels by the interested states, organizations, and intelligentsia and also by the cultural and business circles. In 1988, UNESCO declared their plans of launching the ten year project entitled, "Integral study of the silk route: roads of dialogue". Numerous scientific conferences and seminars were held under the sponsorship of this project. Films were created, books, brochures and articles published and some monuments of archeological and architectural significance were also restored. Creation of folk-ethnographic centers, museums, revival of national trade and crafts centers and educational activities were also intensified.

Specific research activities were initiated to study the *Silk Route* connectivity in India, China, Japan and Srilanka. Again in 1993, at the general assembly of the United Nations (held in Indonesia) a decision was taken to revive the *Silk-Route* as a major channel for the international cooperation. On 7th-8th September 1998, a conference was held in Baku, Azerbaijan to create an international transport corridor for connecting Europe-Caucasus-Asia and an agreement was signed by 32 Countries including Japan, South Korea, China, India and Russia under the Silk Route connectivity project. The agreement included proposals for construction of more than 14000 kms long Trans-Asiatic road to connect the countries in the Atlantic and Pacific Ocean and a possible route map was designed passing from Japan to Turkey and from China to Bulgaria. It was also proposed that a speedway be constructed to connect St. Petersburg with Tokyo and also Helsinki with Khabarovsk. The Asian Development Bank's (ADB) programme for the restoration and revival of the *Silk Route* involved repairing the road-transport trunk connecting Xinjian-Uygur autonomous region of China (Eastern Turkestan) with Central Asia and Iran.[2] The UN development programme (UNDP) in 2001 for the silk route region even aimed to expand the Religious Corporation and development through this route.

The revival of the *Silk Route* connectivity and the transport network is bound to impact economies and the markets positively. The transport linkages can definitely be beneficial for the growth and prosperity of a country but it can also have a disastrous impact and security concerns could increase depending on the situation of the country through which the route passes. New linkages in addition to upgrading existing national and international infrastructures have also been seriously considered in the past few years.[3] As a consequence most of the countries of the region with improved political stability are coming forward with a common agenda of bridging their fragmented networks in order to establish and develop the regional and sub-regional transport system.[4]

Hence, revival of the *Silk Route* connection and development of the transport linkages and network has become a priority for many countries not only in the region but also around the world.

This chapter tries to highlight the significance of the silk route and its connectivity and focuses on the possible transport linkages between India and the Eurasian region. The chapter also tries to bring out the importance of certain connectivity and network specifically for India, giving overview of the regional perspectives. The chapter also focuses on the need to put more attention on certain transport network initiatives to help in increasing the international trade and commerce, for the smooth energy flow and to maintain peace and prosperity in the region.

Regional Transport linkages and Silk Route Network

Presently, in the world there is a growing propensity of interdependency between different social groups, states and regions.[5] Today, the trans-continental transport and communication increased the extent of interdependency of various states and regions and consequently enhances the degree of confidence and security which in return lowers the risk and conflict. The new transport highways are expected to increase human contacts and intensify cultural interactions. However, there is an urgent need to balance economic growth of various regions and narrow down the discrepancy between the advanced and developing countries.

The transport corridors (both road-transport and railways) enables in creating a huge and prosperous market along the routes. Besides, the immense investment allows building transcontinental infrastructure, as well as, creation of thousands of jobs resulting in the economic growth. In the early 20th century, the Trans–Siberian railway line made a great impact on the development of Russian cities such as Omsk, Krasnoyars, Irkutsk, Chita, Khabarovsk, Vladivostok, etc. New transport corridors were developed to integrate Eurasian space into the world economy and boost the modernization process of the regional countries.[6] The pragmatism of such transportation passage is not only to provide opportunities for the economic development but these are the cheapest and swiftest means of exercising delivery of goods and to maintain people to people contact. It is also going to encourage the enactment of common laws for customs and taxation to remove barriers for commodity flow and easing the commercial activities.

Interest in reviving the 'silk route' also enables tourism activities to expand along various roads of the route, since it is one of the most attractive routes and the longest in the World (around 12800 kms). In this respect, a significant role is being played by the World Tourism Organization. According to World Tourism Organisation and UNESCO, the 'silk route' by 2020 is expected to become the most attractive route for the tourists. The countries involved will be able to reap the benefits of huge herbal wealth sprawled over the vast mountainous patches, which will have the potential of revolutionizing the regional *homeopathy* and *ayurvedic medicines* (made from herbs and seeds).[7] It will also help in uniting the divided families and reducing the prevailing tensions on borders thereby decreasing the defence budget and increasing the state's welfare and budget for social security.[8] The *Silk Route* has unique scenic beauty of the sand dunes, hot & cold water gushes, colourful vegetation, multi-coloured hill tops, receding glaciers and a continuous mountain chain on one side while on the other side rivers flow along the roads. The *Silk Route* is expected to help in the integration-transportation-trading and in increasing the cultural connectivity, focusing on the interests of all the concerned countries.[9] Today, it has all possibilities to raise this integration to the highest level with the help of modern technologies to carry forward the greatness of this ancient route in future.

India and the Silk-Route

India has already started renewing the age-old relations with its extended neighbours in Eurasia by reviving some branches of the

Silk Route. India is ideally positioned to expand the volume and direction of land-trade across Eurasia for the economic resurgence of the region. In fact, India has initiated the route revitalization process in view of globalization and free trade.[10] This is essential for the development of the region, however, some potential branches are yet to be revived to realize the regional cooperation and for the overall development.[11]

Nubra Valley in Ladakh is the gateway to Eurasia for India. It has two 'silk route' branches connecting India with Pakistan and China. Both the trade arteries contributed for centuries as an institution of dialogue. The route for Kashmir after crossing Kahardung-La, one of the World's motorable roads, bifurcates near Khalsar. One crosses river Shyok near Tirth and turns northwards almost parallel to Siachen River upto UllanPatiNallah. This stream is a few kms ahead of the Panamik, the hot-spring zone, and just short of Siachen glacier, after which the route turns north-west to cross Saser La reaching Yarkand and other markets of China and the Central Asia region and the Karakoram Pass through Dispang Plain.

Another route moves towards west, parallel to Shyok River, via Diskit-Turkut-Kapalu-Skardu to connect India with Pakistan. This route was used until the mid-20th century; however, it was closed due to the complicated political relationship of India with Pakistan and China. However, it is important to note that these routes were not only used for trade but also used for illegal trade; narco trafficking, spying activities and also for the cross-border terrorism, increasing the security concerns and affecting the development of the region. Though some of these branches have vanished and some have lost their importance, yet there is a wide scope for restoring certain branches in the interest of the stake-holders.

Revival & Regional Developments

It is a known fact that the *Silk Route* is the oldest network known to mankind since 2nd century BC that has played greater role in the regional development. A continuous process of competition to connect the nations and regions at appropriate interceptions throughout its evolution also made it a complete communication network system and became 'road of dialogue'. Unfortunately, its demise was so quick that most of the traces of the glorious past were eradicated. The 'silk route' is now renewed in new fashion with new interest and loyalties and it is expected to play a major role in the regional cooperation. Revival of the route will help in the peaceful co-existence and address the regional security threats too.

Significant Routes

The *Leh-Panamik-Yarkand route*, the northern route connecting Ladakh with Yarkand and other cities of China & Central Asia via Karakoram always remained a route of choice for caravans as there were two sub-routes which made the travelling possible. During the Dogra rule (1846-1947) in Kashmir, the government allocated a specific annual budget for the maintenance of this route. Hence, *sarias* (motels) and other facilities were developed at various spots where traders received supplies for men and animals. Dominated by Buddhist settlements, the villages had the longitudinal sprawl along the roads. The population and stock densities were mostly dependent on the availability of water in the nearby area. Even today, all along the road there exist grave yards of Yarkandies (khojas) and other ill-fated traders and travellers. The emotional attachment has always played a significant role here. The continuation of growing crops and preserving wild fruits cherished by caravans and multi-cut fodder variety were consumed by animals which could still be found in these areas which also depicts preservation of the sentimental values. Hence, reopening of these routes will elevate the economic condition as well as, they will even connect people of various races and colours.

Another significant route is *Leh-Turtuk-Skardu route*, after leaving Shyok-Siachen confluence near Diskit, the western route goes parallel to Shyok River taking its west bank upto Thang. Here it is joined by another trade artery coming from Leh via Skiribichan after crossing Chorbat La, it crisscrosses the Shyok to enter through Khapalu. A fully metallic road safe for two-way vehicular movement on smooth gradient, this route runs along the foothills and some of the oldest settlements are located along this route. During the glorious period of trade, in order to ease the access to supply lines for both human and animals this was very prominent road connection. Many villages were located near this route in summer but shifted to the lower foothills during winter to avoid extreme cold and snow storms. It is known that it'll be indeed beneficial and interesting for all the countries concerned to revive the silk route for economic and trade prospects. However, this promising opportunity needs to be redeemed. All the three basic components i.e. geographical proximity, technological feasibility and economic viability favours the revival.[12] There has to be proper access between or among the countries for economic integration and regional cooperation. Some of the landlocked developing countries face tough time exporting their products and as a result they trade less and grow slowly in comparison to their coastal neighbours. There are also other problems faced by the landlocked countries such as border delays due to multiple clearance processes, security problems and weak custom administration and corruption. All these also contribute to the artificially hiked transport costs.[13] Thus, regional cooperation in improving the connectivity plays a significant role in bringing down these gaps while same time, promoting economic integration.[14] Most of the countries of the region today with improved political stability are coming forward with a common agenda for establishing and developing the regional and sub-regional transport system.[15]

Significant Regional Transport Corridors

There are number of transport corridors developing in the Eurasian region connecting the countries with each other. Both the energy and transport route especially passing through the Eurasian states of Central Asia and Caucasus has been receiving considerable attention through the development policies of East-West corridor connections where, the Eurasian states are linked with the South & East Asia moving towards the Europe. Today, there exists plethora of regional transport network systems, such as the Black Sea Pan-European transport Area, the European cooperation initiative, Black Sea Economic Co-operation (BSEC), Europe's Transport Corridor in the Europe-Caucasus-Asia (TRACECA) project and so on. However, the initial thrust for improving the trade route has been more or less in a horizontal nature along the East-West corridor.

One of the Corridors is Europe-Caucasus-Asia corridor (TRACECA). The TRACECA may be referred to as the renaissance of the great *Silk Route*. TRACECA is the technical assistance programme for development of the transport corridor between Europe and Asia across the Black Sea. The countries of the South Caucasus, the Caspian Sea and the Central Asian countries are involved in the development of this corridor. The TRACECA programme was launched in May 1993, since then EU has financed 62 technical assistance and 14 investments projects.[16]

In September 1998, twelve countries (Armenia, Azerbaijan, Bulgaria, Georgia, Kazakhstan, Kyrgyzstan, Moldova, Romania, Tajikistan, Turkey, Uzbekistan and Ukraine) signed the "Basic Multilateral Agreement on International Transport for the Development of the Transport Corridor Europe-Caucasus-Asia", comprising four supplementary technical annexes on rail and road transport and commercial maritime navigation.

TRACECA aims at supporting political and economic independence of the states by enhancing their capacity to access European markets and World markets through alternative transport routes, encouraging further regional co-operation among the partner countries. TRACECA helps in assisting in the development of economic relations, trade and transport communications in Europe, in the Black Sea region and in Asia. It ensures access to the world market through road and rail transport and commercial navigation, ensuring traffic security, cargo safety and environmental protection. TRACECA harmonizes the transport policy and legal structure in the field of transport and creates good conditions for transport cooperation. Increasingly, TRACECA is trying to attract the support of International Financial Institutions (IFIs) and private investors. TRACECA desires to deliver a sustainable, efficient and integrated multimodal transport system.[17]

Regional Transport Network Initiatives

Due to increase in the volume of trade and commercial interaction in the region, there are many more routes under construction and are almost ready to take-off. One such route is BTC Pipeline (the second longest oil pipeline of the former Soviet Union). Though BTC operates mainly for connecting West with the Caucasian region, nonetheless, there is a possibility of establishing BTC's connectivity with the TAPI (Turkmenistan-Afghanistan-Pakistan-India) pipeline. TAPI is envisaged to bring energy from Daulatabad-Herat-Kandahar-Quetta-Multan to Fazilka in the North Indian state of Punjab. The 1800 km. length pipeline is estimated to cost 9 billion USD and has a capacity to carry 90 million metric standard cubic meters/day of gas for 30 years. India and Pakistan have agreed on a uniform transit fee and it seems Pakistan has mentioned that it will accept whatever India and Afghanistan agrees upon. India has also recently approved the "Special Purpose Vehicle" (SPV) for TAPI. India's GAIL has made an initial investment of 5 million USD for TAPI project. Of late, Bangladesh has also shown interest in joining the TAPI project. TAPI plans to start the operations by 2017. The revival of economic and trade activities through regional transport networks will contribute in enhancing the regional cooperation. The development of these routes will connect the States of Eurasia with India more closely and in the process this will enhance the infrastructure of the region.

The Trans-Siberian Railway (TSR) is often associated with the main trans-continental Russian line that connects many large and small cities of the Eurasian region. The Trans-Siberian Railways are also known as the spinal cord of Russia connecting Moscow with Vladivostok and is the longest railway-route in the World. It covers seven times zones and takes eight days to complete the journey. It is the third longest single continuous service in the world and is in operation since 1916 and even today it is expanding and modernization process is still continuing. The main route of the Trans-Siberian Railways begins in Moscow at YaroslavskyVokzal, runs through Yaroslav, Chelyabinks, Omsk, Novosibirsk, Irkutsk, Ulan-Ude, Chita and Khabarovsk to Vladivostok via Southern Siberia. The construction of TSR was started in the year 1891 and was complete in the year 1916 and for decades it has been the principle railway link between European Russia and its industrial regions towards the East i.e. Urals (most part of Urals lies in Russia and also some part of the Ural region lies in north western Kazakhstan)-Barnaul-Altai-Khakassia-Tuva-Irkutsk-Buryatia-Chita.[18] The TSR is 9,288 km long and was fully electrified by the year 2002. Its several lines in the far eastern section are linked with China, North Korea and with the railways connections of Mongolia. It is also well connected with the Central Asian railways and with the Western European railways via Belarus. At present the TSR is technically capable of carrying 250-300 thousand equivalent units (TEU's) of the international transit cargoes per-annum. However, it is expected that once the modernisation of the TSR is complete and if the Baikal-Amur Mainline (BAM) railway starts functioning, then this figure will increase by 1 million TEU's per annum. Russian railways have already thought of investing 50 billion rubles i.e. approximately 1.5 billion USD for the modernisation process of TSR, primarily to allow it to handle special containers.

Another significant development is taking place in the Kazakh-Chinese pipeline construction work. This is China's first direct oil import pipeline from Central Asia. There is also the volume of truck trade going on between Afghanistan, Pakistan and Iran. Recently India has also struck a deal with Afghanistan to exploit the iron ores in the Hajigak mines of Afghanistan, (estimated to be around 1.3 trillion USD). Now India is building roads developing the connectivity and linkages with Afghanistan for easy accessibility and developing trade and economic cooperation. India has already invested around 136 million USD to link Chabahar port of Iran to Afghanistan by roads. India has also developed a new highway Zeranj-Delaram Highway in Afghanistan linking this route with Afghanistan's renewed ring road at Herat. India has also proposed to join the project of connecting Iran's Banzar-Anzali on the Caspian coast to Russia.[19] In the wake of such large stakes, India is forthright in developing its connectivity through transport corridors for overcoming its biggest drawback of the lack of connectivity in the region.

Asian Highway Network

The Asian Highway Network is a network of 141,000 kilometers of standardized roadways crisscrossing 32 Asian countries linking Europe. The Asian Highway project was initiated in the year 1959 with the aim of promoting the development of international road transport in the region. During the first phase of the project (1960-1970) considerable progress was achieved, however, progress slowed down when financial assistance was suspended in 1975.[20]In 1980's and 1990's, regional political and economic changes spurred new momentum for the Asian Highway Project. It became one of the three pillars of Asian Land Transport Infrastructure Development (ALTID) project, endorsed by ESCAP Commission at its forty-eighth session in 1992, comprising of Asian Highway, Trans-Asian Railway and for the facilitation of the land transport projects.[21]

The Intergovernmental Agreement on the Asian Highway Network was adopted on 18th November 2003, by an inter-governmental meeting held in Bangkok and entered into force on 4th July 2005. A total of US$26 billion has already been invested for the improvement and upgradation of the Asian Highway network. United Nations Economic and Social Commission for the Asia and Pacific (UNESCAP) secretariat is now working with the member countries to identify financial sources for the development of network to improve the road transport capacity and efficiency.[22]

International North South Corridor (INSTC)

The North-South Transport Corridor is a term used to describe the ship, rail, and road route for moving freight from South Asia to Europe through Central Asia, the Caucasus and Russia. The route primarily involves moving goods from India via ship to Iran. From Iran, the freight moves by ship across the Caspian Sea or by truck or rail to Southern Russia. From there, the goods are transported by truck or rail along the Volga River through Moscow to Northern Europe. In 2001, Russia, Iran and India signed an agreement to further develop the route. India has taken a major step in arranging the meeting of the countries including Iran, Russia and the countries of Central Asia, as well as Bulgaria, to push the idea of this project and its implementation. Currently, the project includes countries such as Azerbaijan, Armenia, Kazakhstan, Kyrgyzstan, Tajikistan, Turkey, Ukraine, Belarus and Oman, besides the countries mentioned earlier. One of the major partners in this project is Iran.[23] The political differences between the countries did not deter the intention of India or other interested partners in this project to continue with this project for its success.

India's active interest to pursue the project is due to variety of considerations. Indian goods reach Russia and Central Asia travelling through long routes of Suez Canal. This project envisages a multi-modal transportation network that connects ports on India's west coast to Bandar Abbas in Iran, then overland to Bandar Anzali port on the Caspian Sea. Through Rasht and Astara on the Azerbaijan border onwards to Kazakhstan and further towards

Russia and through Mediterranean to the Ukrainian ports of Odessa and Kiev and then onwards to Russia and Central Asia. This route also has the rail connectivity of about 200 km from Iran to the Caspian Sea. This network can be further expanded to Europe and towards the South East Asia.[24] The new route will reduce transport cost and travel time to a significant extent. While the Suez Canal route takes about 45-60 days, the Iran route will take about 25-30 days. The India-Russia-Iran cordial relationship is likely to help in realising this project in expected time. Another reason why India is interested to pursue this route via Iran is due to India's unfriendly relationship with Pakistan and the turmoil in Afghanistan.

The larger implications of the North-South corridor, which has also other branches such as the route linking Turkmenistan and Azerbaijan or the route linking Afghanistan and Uzbekistan both of which can be linked to this corridor, will have wider significance for the region. It will help in opening up vast markets in India, Russia and Central Asia and in other parts of Asia and Europe too. The Customs Union of the countries of Russia, Ukraine and Belarus can be further expanded and linked to other countries of Eurasia as well as to India in order to have wider economic entity, which can use this transport corridor for easy and better connectivity.[25] This energy rich region with vast geography and with vast resources is expected to play a crucial role in the emerging new great game in the post-Soviet Eurasian space. The politico-economic dimension of this route will be significant in the international political scenario with the indications of shift in the global power base.

The North-South Corridor will help to develop a web of bilateral infrastructure for trade routes in the region and for the flow of goods and people, otherwise impeded at the borders due to the lack of bilateral and multi-lateral agreements. It will also reduce the transportation costs(otherwise it creates big hindrance which stem from variations in technical and legal requirements such as vehicle weights, dimensions and operating permits, inconsistent documentation and inspections etc.) The rail corridor connecting Northern Europe with Helsinki as the reference point of origin with ports in the Persian Gulf with Bandar Abbas as the reference destination port is the backbone for a distinctive distance advantage over the existing shipping route. The Helsinki to Bandar Abbas distance by sea is around 7,217 nautical miles, i.e. 13,366 km.[26] In other words, the corridor would nearly reduce the distance by half.

The countries concerned would have to define a set of common technical standards and make available the necessary financial resources to implement them so that there is a speedy activation of movement. Sufficient resources are to be allocated to ensure the least possible level of impediment for smooth operation of transit. Currently the only existing continuous all-rail operation between Helsinki and Bandar Abbas is via Central Asian route through Russia, Kazakhstan, Uzbekistan and Turkmenistan, (7,549-km) long route via Taxiatash or the (7,885km) long route via Nukuss. The Caspian Sea route is the shortest of all routes within the corridors.[27]

The Eurasian States have shown keen interest in opening up the network of routes in the region. Russia, Uzbekistan and Kazakhstan President's during their visits to India emphasized on the need to increase cooperation and connectivity between the regional countries, as close network and linkages can bring the countries of the region in mutually beneficial framework and will also have the potential to reduce the rivalry between them. In today's geo-political scenario, better connectivity and better trade and economic relationship is extremely important. The north-south corridor will certainly facilitate this prospect and bring the powers of the region together and increase mutual understanding and cooperation.

Conclusion

Revival of the *Silk Route* connectivity and development of the transport corridors and improving the linkages will increase the regional cooperation and can be considered as a major tool for transport and trade developments. There are major markets that surround these land-locked countries of Eurasia, which can be connected easily through these viable routes. Regional cooperation agreement helps in removing many potential obstacles. Transport Corridors can indeed contribute significantly in developing trade and transit among the regional Countries. The significance of revival of Silk Route and the transport corridor developing in the region would be to provide a platform to improve cooperation as well as the communications and reduce barriers to permit the economies of each country to grow independently and achieve objectives for the benefit of the country and the region as a whole.

End Notes

1 Alan Lee Boyer, *Recreating the Silk Road: The Challenges of overcoming transaction costs*, China and Eurasia Vol. IV, No.4, Central Asia- Caucasus Institute and Silk Route Studies Programme, 2006, pp.72-74.

2 Richard Foltz, *Religions of the Silk Road*, Palgrave Macmillan, New York, 2nd edition, 2010

3 C.M. Hogan, Burnham A. ed. *Silk Road, North China, the Megalithic Portal and Megalith Map*, http://www.megalithic.co.uk/article. php?sid=18006. 13th July, 2011

4 Boulnois Luce, *Silk Road: Monks, Warriors & Merchants*, Odyssey Books, Hong Kong, 2005, p. 66.

5 Jaspers K, *Sense and Perpouse of History*, Moscow, 1994, p.141.

6 *The Silk Roads: Highways of Culture and Commerce*, UNESCO Publication,Berghahn Book, 2001

7 Ash Narain Roy, *A Corridor of Prosperity*, available at www. hardnewsmedia.com.

8 G.M. Mir, *"Resource management, regional cooperation and sustainable development states"*, New Delhi, 2003.

9 Asia-Pacific | Asia takes first step on modern 'Silk Route'". BBC News. 05.01. 2013.

10 Asia-Pacific | Asia takes first step on modern 'Silk Route'". BBC News. 05.01. 2013.

11 Eliseeff, "Approaches Old and New to the Silk Roads" in *The Silk Roads: Highways of Culture and Commerce*, Paris, 1998, UNESCO, Reprinted Berghahn Books, 2009, pp. 1–2.

12 David Gosset, *"Xinjiang and the revival of Silk Route"*, Greater China, 2000.

13 Hussain Moazzen, Lyan lur Islam, Reza kibra, *South Asian Economic development: transformation opportunities and challenges*, Routledge, London, New York, 1999.

14 World Bank Report, *From Disintegration to Reintegration: Europe and Central Asia in International Trade,*2006, available at http://www. worldbank.org/.

15 S.Polanchek, *Conflict and Trade*, Journal of Conflict Resolution, Vol. 24 (1)1980, pp.55-78.

16 Wilfred J.Ethier, *Regionalism in a multilateral World*, Journal of Political Economy, Vol.106 (6) December, 1998, pp.1214-12145.

17 *Silk Road*, http://www.livius.org/sh-si/silk_road/silk_road.html, LIVIUS Articles of Ancient History, 28 October 2010.

18 Seehttp://ec.europa.eu/europeaid/where/asia/regional-cooperation-central asia/transport/traceca_en.htm.

19 World Bank Report, *From Disintegration to re-integration: Europe and Central Asia in International Trade*, 2006, available at http://www. worldbank.Org.

20 ibid.

21 Ibid. Ash Narain Roy, *A Corridor of Prosperity*, available at www.hardnewsmedia.com.

22 Ulric Killion, *A Modern Chinese Journey to the West: Economic Globalization and Dualism*, Nova Science Publishers, 2006, p.66.

23 United Nation development Programme (UNDP), Human Development Report, 2994: Cultural library in today's diverse world," UNDP, New York 2004.

24 http://www.unescap.org/ttdw/index.asp?menuname=asianhighway

25 Waugh, Daniel. Richthofen's "Silk Roads: Toward the Archaeology of a Concept." *The Silk Road*. Volume 5, Number 1, Summer 2007, p. 4.

26 *World Bank: trade and transport facilitation in Central Asia: Reducing the economic distance to markets"*, Final draft Report, 2005. *Russia-India Report*, RIA Novosti Publication, Moscow, 2012.

27 North South Corridor", Times of India Report, 13 March 2012, United Nations Economic and Social Commissions for Asia and the Pacific, *"Transit Transport Issue in Landlocked and transit Developing Countries"*, Report No.ST/ESCAP/2270, 2003Jean Francois Arvis, *"Transit and the Special Case of landlocked Countries, Customs Mordernization Hand Book, Luc De Wulf and Jose B.Sokol*, the World bank, Washington, DC, 2005.

References

Prevas John, *Envy of the Gods: Alexander the Great's Ill-Fated Journey across Asia*, De Capo Press, Cambridge, 2004, p121.

Jerry H. Bentley,*Old World Encounters: Cross-Cultural Contacts and Exchanges in Pre-Modern Times,*New York: Oxford University Press, 1993,p. 32, 38-37,43-48.

Dybo A.V., *Chronology of Türkic languages and linguistic contacts of early Türks*, Moscow, 2007, p. 786.

Wink André, *Al-Hind: The Making of the Indo-Islamic World*, Brill Academic Publishers, 2002.

Hays J.N., *Epidemics and pandemics: their impacts on human history*, 2005, p.61.

Arbrey, Patricia Buckley; Anne Walthall and James B. Palais, *East Asia: A Cultural, Social, and Political History*, Houghton Mifflin, 2nd revised edition 2008, p. 257.

Yang Bin, *Between Winds and Clouds: The Making of Yunnan*. New York: Columbia University Press,2008.

Foltz Richard C., *Religions of the Silk Road: Overland Trade and Cultural Exchange from Antiquity to the Fifteenth Century*. New York: St Martin's Press, 1999, pp. 37-47.

WTO Data Base of 7th November 2012.

Michel Sims, *Harmonization and simplification of transport agreements, cross-border documents and transport regulations*, Report Prepared for the Asian development bank, Manila 2005.

Ian Jenkins and Paul Pezant, *Central Asia: Reassessment of the Regional Transport Sector Strategy*, A Report prepared for the Asian Development Bank, Manila, 2003.

3

Energy Security and the Development Strategies

Relevance of Eurasia is on rise, the region has major stakes in the geopolitics of oil and gas, security and power dynamics of the region. The wider region of Eurasia is increasingly visible in today's world politico-economic scenario. The region being situated in between East and West is also prone to instability, conflict and poverty, which is affecting the security of the region.[1] The same factors coupled with the slow development of the political systems, also fueled radicalism security threats and concerns. The previous chapters of this book have debated on a range of interconnected political, diplomatic, economic and strategic issues that are emerging between India & Eurasia. This chapter discusses the security commonalities and on the strategy formulations between India and the Eurasian states.

India being an important player in Asia with stable economy is growing its engagement with the Eurasian States. The issues related to development strategies includes energy cooperation, transportation and regional developments which are central issues linked with the development of dynamic foreign policy imperatives, enabling technologies and security issues to move simultaneously. Today, the obvious path adopted for tackling such issues in the Eurasian region is through regional cooperation.

For debating the security challenges it is important to appreciate the dynamics of bilateral and multilateral relationships and also inter-state and intra-state relationships. Political and economic rivalry and competition among the states also needs to be factored in to gauge security challenges.

The power politics of Eurasia is dominated by Russia and its pre-eminence is unquestionable. Russia is involved in a leading capacity in all major hydroelectric power projects in the region. The main trade routes from Central Asia cross Russian Federation so naturally the importance of Russia could not be overlooked. Theoretically, it could be argued that new corridors planned to open via Iran, Afghanistan and Pakistan will be much more economically viable and prospective for the region but for political or security reasons the routes passing through these countries will have many security implications.[2] As regards to the involvement of foreign oil companies in crude oil reserves mainly in Central Asia is concerned, North American companies rank top in Kazakhstan, with almost half of reserves, followed by companies from Russia, Italy, UK and China. The distribution of ownership of gas reserves is somewhat more complex. Many of the Kazakh reserves belong to Euro-American companies and Turkmen reserves to Russian or Chinese companies. Off late, Eurasian energy issues are becoming a point of tensions for relations between Russia and The United States.[3] It is becoming increasingly difficult for US and Russia to work together in the region. Russia's perception is that it is being encircled, while the US's standpoint is that stable democracies on Russia's borders are essential as well as beneficial for the whole region. Furthermore, the US perspective holds that democracy and stability are necessary for further development of the Eurasian region and that this stability is vital for the Euro-Atlantic security sphere. On the other hand, Russia is repeatedly and increasingly using energy politics as an extension of foreign policy. However, Russia's advantage is that oil or gas extracted from the region is almost all transported through its territory. This Chapter focuses on the potential of the region and security concerns that are attached with it and also possible cooperation and convergence in formulating development strategies policies.

Energy and Hydropower Security

India today is the world's fifth largest consumer of energy. If India's economy continues to grow even at the modest rate of 5 to 6 per cent annually it will lead to a sharp increase in India's energy requirements over the next two to three decades. Efficient and reliable energy supplies are a precondition for sustaining India's economic growth. As India grows, its population will also grow and become more urbanized, more mobile and more prosperous, making India a voracious consumer of energy. The Integrated Energy Policy (IEP) report of the India's Planning Commission, released in 2006, estimates that by 2031-32 India's primary energy demand will triple.[4]

Currently, India's primary energy mix is dominated by coal (51 per cent), followed by oil (36 per cent), natural gas (10 per cent), hydropower (2 per cent), and nuclear energy (1 per cent). Under any scenario the overall energy mix will continue to be dominated by coal, oil and gas for the next quarter century. Hydropower, nuclear energy and renewable sources of energy like wind, solar, bio-fuels and hydrogen can continue marginally but are not critical to India's energy security. The Integrated Energy Policy realistically concludes that even with a concerted push and a 40 fold increase in their contribution to primary energy, renewable sources of energy may account for only 5 to 6 per cent of India's energy mix by 2031-32.[5]

Amongst renewable sources of energy, hydropower is perhaps the most significant source. The Energy Policy of the government clarifies that even if India succeeds in exploiting its full hydro potential of 150,000 MW, the contribution of hydro energy to the energy mix will only be around 1.9-2.2 per cent.[6]

The share of hydropower in India's energy mix could significantly increase if in addition to India's own hydropower the potential of Tajikistan and Kyrgyzstan could be tapped. India is continuing its energy diplomacy and negotiations with its Eurasian neighbours in this regard and this cooperation will also fulfill the non-energy benefits. Nonetheless, Political will and security concerns are the key to the success of such cooperation which need to be addressed carefully.

Fossil Fuels Significance

Over the next quarter century, the share of oil and gas in total energy consumption is expected to be at least 45 per cent in the overall energy mix. Growing urbanization and rapid development of the transport sector will drive the demand for oil. Gas used primarily by the power of fertilizer sector (80 per cent) and to a lesser degree by the transport and household sectors. Natural gas-fed power plants are less expensive per kilowatt of the electricity generated with higher thermal efficiency; they also have a shorter construction period than oil or coal-based power plants.[7]Unfortunately, India's indigenous oil and gas production has reached a plateau. Despite the discovery of the new gas fields in the Krishna-Godavari basin in the Bay of Bengal, the additional output from these sources will contribute only marginally for bridging the supply-demand gap in the coming years. Hence, India's continued heavy dependency on imported oil and gas is inescapable.

In order to diversify its sources of oil supplies, as well as to ensure that India's imported oil dependency does not go beyond the existing level, India has embarked on a policy of making equity investments in oilfields abroad. In the last few years Indian oil companies, both publicly and privately owned have made significant investments in the oilfields as well as in the exploration blocks in the States of the Eurasian region, mainly in Russia and in Central Asia. Such measures will certainly help in getting assured supplies for providing energy security to India and maintaining the continuity of such measures.

Energy Projects

One of the significant projects between India and Eurasia in the recent period is the Turkmenistan-Afghanistan-Pakistan-India (TAPI) pipeline project. Amidst rising instability and violence in the region progress on the Turkmenistan, Afghanistan, Pakistan and India gas pipeline project gave new hope for bringing peace & stability in the region. The projected gains from the pipeline are seen as an opportunity to create new possibilities for regional stakeholders. The TAPI pipeline will boost economic interdependency among competing regional powers. In early 1990's TAPI natural gas pipeline was first proposed, then in 1995, this project was signed between Turkmenistan and Pakistan. In 1998, project was stopped due to conflict and the unsettled political situation in Afghanistan. Again in 2001, fall of the Taliban regime opened new opportunities to revive the project. In 2003, Technical Assistance Plan was formed for a Turkmenistan-Afghanistan-Pakistan (TAP) pipeline. In 2005, feasibility study for the pipeline was done and in 2008, India after receiving cabinet's approval officially joined TAPI. In December 2010's Ashgabat summit of the four (TAPI) states gave a new impetus to the TAPI project. In December 2010, Turkmen, Afghan, Pakistan and Indian leaders signed two key agreements- (1) Inter-governmental Agreement, (2) The Gas Pipeline Transmission Agreement. Agreements foresee 33 billion cubic meters (bcm) of natural gas flow through the TAPI pipeline each year. Out of which 3 bcm allocated for use in Afghanistan, 15 bcm each for Pakistan and India.[8]

The TAPI pipeline strategy from Turkmenistan's Dauletabad gas fields before passing through Herat and Kandahar will follow Afghanistan's Ring Road. The pipeline would extend to the cities of Quetta and Multan in Pakistan and connect to the Indian city of Fazilka at the Indo-Pak border. Its total length would be approximately 1,735km. The $10 billion, TAPI pipeline's first supplies are planned for 2017.[9] TAPI pipeline offers benefits to all four participating countries and has the potential to enhance regional cooperation. Turkmenistan, currently exports gas only to Russia, however, this project will provide alternatives to Turkmenistan for exporting its energy resources to other Countries of the region too. Pakistan and India will be able to use Turkmen gas to address their current energy deficits. Regionally, TAPI pipeline will provide new business opportunities for the gas and engineering industries.

ADB (Asian Development Bank) is leading stakeholder of this project. Oil and gas firms such as Chevron, Exxon, Gazprom and GAIL are part of the project. There will be difficulty in protecting TAPI pipeline in conflict affected regions of Afghanistan. However, Afghan National Army will face challenges in defending the TAPI pipeline. Afghan government promised to provide minimum 7,000 security personnel to guard the pipeline in Afghanistan alone, though there is a fear that the pipeline might face severe security threat if the on-going insurgency continues.[10] TAPI pipeline poses significant potential for improving energy security and regional integration. The four countries involved needs to have the strong will to realise the project, but it remains to be seen whether they will be successful in overcoming challenges related to pricing, gas certification, technical capacity, funding and security concerns. TAPI gas pipeline project across Afghanistan is expected to help to stabilize Afghanistan by generating much-needed income and jobs in that country and would go a long way in persuading the youth to turn away from insurgency and in the process a stable and united Afghanistan will help to provide security guarantees to the region.

Another significant upcoming project is CASA i.e. the Central Asia-South Asia Electricity Trade and Transmission Project more commonly known as CASA-1000 is under consideration to aid Afghanistan and Pakistan in importing electricity from Tajikistan and Kyrgyzstan.[11] In India several offshore gas fields have been discovered in the Bay of Bengal which could help India meet its energy needs. Another important development in connecting the regional countries together is on the "International North South Corridor", on February 22, 1997, Transport corridor agreement was first signed between India, Iran and Turkmenistan. On March 29, 2012, 14 stakeholders signed the final agreement on "International North-South Corridor" in New Delhi. This project will link the Indian port of Mumbai with the Iranian Bandar Abbas terminal, through which the containers move across Iranian port of Mashshad and Sarakhs to Tejen in Turkmenistan and further moving to east across the Turkmen cities Mary and Turkmenabat to Bukhara – Navoy – Samarkand and Tashkent in Uzbekistan and reaches Rasht and Astara on the Azerbaijan border to other Central Asian states of Kazakhstan, Kyrgyzstan and Tajikistan and further moves towards Russia. This route connect Europe and Asia in a unique way --- estimated distance could be covered in 25-30 days what currently takes 45-60 days through the Suez Canal.[12] This Corridor will open-up new markets and could be used to transport oil, gas, uranium and other industrial goods too. INSTC will boost-up trade and economic cooperation between India and the Eurasian states. All these innovative projects have been going on for many years now. India got involved in these projects for the purpose of fulfilling its energy security needs as well as for political and strategic considerations.

Policy and Approach for Eurasian Connectivity

In the Eurasian region Russia and China have strong presence. India needs to understand the security aspects and the energy policy dynamics of the Eurasian States. Any energy pipeline from Eurasia to India that does not cross Afghanistan/Pakistan possibly could be routed via Xinjiang and then across the Karakoram and the Himalayan mountain ranges. Apart from the considerable technical challenges, the political obstacles to such an alignment are likely to be more daunting, since the pipeline route would have to be laid across the disputed Aksai Chin area between India and China. An India-China understanding on the pipeline across Aksai Chin is essential, however, if the two countries agree then such a project would be able to bring significant long-term energy and strategic benefits to both these nations as well as to the Central Asian States.

There is a proposal that a gas pipeline across the Karakorm-Himalaya ranges could lead to the development of a major energy corridor between Eurasia and the Indian Ocean. Oil pipeline too could be built along the same alignment, with the oil flowing in the opposite direction. In the process would be technically much more challenging. It is much easier to transport gas which is lighter than oil at high altitudes and at low temperature.[13]This project could be of great interest to both India and China. India could offer a similar transit oil corridor too. The Indian transit route may not only turn out to be more secure and technically feasible, but have the advantage of creating a mutual dependence that is mainly Chinese dependence on India for transit of Gulf oil destined for China and India's dependence on China for transit of Eurasian gas destined for India. In the process would get assured energy supplies for their own domestic needs and become central to the energy flows out of Eurasia. Even though China and India are the competitors in receiving the global energy resources, India and China do share a long-term interest for fulfilling their energy demands with the available energy resources from the Eurasian region. To ensure this, both China and India would have to come together and use their clout as big and growing consumers of energy in the region. If they work jointly then they can offer a viable and more secure pipeline route. Energy corridor could also bring both China and India significant non-energy benefits. China could earn sizeable pipeline transit fees. Investments for pipeline projects could provide employment opportunities and stimulate Xinjiang and Western Tibet's economic development and contribute to their stability.

The gains to India from the Eurasian-Indian pipeline projects would be many-fold. Availability of a cheap and plentiful clean energy source like gas would go a long way towards resolving growing problems of deforestation and environmental degradation in the Himalayas. In this process Jammu & Kashmir could benefit enormously from a re-opening of its traditional links with Xinjiang and Western Tibet via Ladakh.[14] These types of major joint energy projects, pipelines, would give an enormous boost to the economic activities and this might also be able to bring-up suitable conditions for initiating the political dialogue.

Another option for the successful Eurasian energy project is trilateral close cooperation i.e. if Russia-India-China, three countries together agrees in principle to have a strategic cooperation in the field of energy. Perhaps this could constitute a concrete project within the Russia-India-China-(RIC) trilateral framework or through the Shanghai Cooperation Orgnisation (SCO) forum too.

Energy Security & Cooperation

India's rapid economic growth and industrialization has drawn world attention and it is being perceived as one of the major Asian power. In order to sustain a steady pace of growth, it is vital for India to ensure a timely and an uninterrupted supply of energy. With developed and developing countries both competing for energy resource, the issue of energy security acquired a critical dimension in the international politics.[15] Given the heavy dependency on imports, the energy security issues have become a key concern for India. Today ensuring energy security has become an integral component of Indian foreign policy and diplomacy. The rising demand for energy and the politicization of the energy issue complicated the energy scenario. In order to smoothen the energy supplies, the Indian government has encouraged its Public Sector Units (PSU) and Gas authority of India limited (GAIL) to acquire stakes/equity in oil and gas fields abroad.[16]

Russia is India's trusted strategic partner and is destined to play a vital role in ensuring India's energy security in the coming decades. India is energy deficient country and Russia is energy surplus and therefore, a mutual interest lies in this sector. India's policy makers are trying to promote energy cooperation based on political understanding. Indian side feels that there is a clear compatibility between India's needs and Russia's resources. Indian side is adopting a policy to implement the experience of Sakhalin-1 to other oilfields in Russia.

The former Soviet Union played a major role in building India's energy sector by building hydropower stations, developing India's coal industry, finding oil in Indian soil and helping in setting up India's energy major Oil and Natural gas Company (ONGC). Indo-Russian energy cooperation acquired new dimensions in the post-Soviet period, particularly in the hydrocarbon and nuclear sector. India has invested $2.8 billion in the Sakhalin energy project, controlling 20% stakes in the venture and has purchased Imperial Energy, (London-listed oil major in Tomks region). These are India's largest investments abroad. (Nord Imperial, a subsidiary of Imperial Energy, has been among the companies that submitted applications to bid for developing Russia's Trebs and Titov oil deposits in the Arctic). India has been eying energy projects at Timon Pechora basin and Vancour in the East Siberia. India is also considering an option to invest $1.5 billion to $1.7 billion for an opportunity in Yamal peninsula that houses one-fifth of global natural gas reserves, offered by Russian firm Navatek. Russia's 'Project Yenisey' involves an upstream hydrocarbon block-linked natural gas liquefaction project and liquefied natural gas marketing. The Indian state-run energy majors that are exploring the possibility of having a strong footing in Russia's energy sector include ONGC, GAIL and Petronet LNG. GAIL plans to invest Rs 7000-8000 crore in Yamal-Nanets region and has the option to market the LNG or even bring back that to India. Novatek has a 51% stake in OAO Yamal LNG, which has the licence for exploration and development of the South Tambeyskoye field located in the northeast of the Yamal peninsula.[17]India's policy is to promote the idea of India's willingness to offer Russian companies to participate in Indian oil and gas projects, both in upstream and downstream, as well as to undertake joint exploration in other countries too.

Indian side feels that though Russia and India are not geographically contiguous there is no hindrance for cooperation since the international oil and gas trade is not based on contiguity. India's interest in the Russian energy sector has already been proved by India's investment in Sakhalin-1. While public sector energy companies from India have already made considerable investments in Russia, now India is also promoting its private sector companies for investments in downstream petroleum units in Russia in return for a stake in petroleum refineries there.[18]India has proposed an exploration venture with Russian gas majors Gazprom and Rosneft and sought a stake in the Sakhalin-III oil and gas project in the Far East. India is also now entering Russia's Sakhalin IV project. Indian side has proposed joint venture to work on gas liquefactions projects in Russian offshore fields for Shipment to India.[19]

India is also looking for options for transporting Russian crude to India through a pipeline link from Xinjiang to India. But this depends on a joint agreement between Russia-Kazakhstan-China-India. The proposal is such, that crude from Russia could be transported via 1,240 kilometer long pipeline from Atasu in northwest Kazakhstan to China's Xinjiang province. This pipeline could enter the Xinjiang province in China at Altay, climb the Tianshan Mountain and extend southward to the Kunlun Mountains in India.[20]

India's ONGC has proposed another energy highway to construct a Russia-China-India (RCI) pipeline. The RCI is supposed to stretch from Russia through Turkmenistan,

Uzbekistan, Kazakhstan, to Kashgar in China's Xinjiang. It could enter India via Ladakh, crossing the Siachen glaciers and the India-China Line of Control or alternatively through Himachal Pradesh to supply gas to Northern India. The proposed pipeline would extend over an extremely long stretch of varied terrain and the study showed that construction of the pipeline may cost somewhere up to $15 billion, or slightly less if connected through already operating pipelines.[21]

Tatarstan's energy company, (one of the most economically developed regions in Russia), and Reliance Industries Limited's (RIL) have agreed to set up a joint working group of specialists to develop strategic partnership in petrochemical and oil refining sectors, specially in crude oil refining.[22]

Russia's energy strategy towards Asia clearly mentions India as one of the important target countries along with Japan, China and Korea. India is carefully taking note of Russia's hydrocarbon vision as India wants to have a strong presence in Russia's massive energy sector that can help ensure India's vital energy security.[23] Amidst all these developments there is a hope that India-Russia energy cooperation will scale towards new heights in the coming years.

Kazakhstan has emerged as one of the major economies in Central Asia. Kazakhstan has large exportable resources of hydrocarbons, coal and uranium. India-Kazakhstan energy cooperation can provide energy security to India too. India on its part can provide a vast market for Kazakhstan's oil and mineral resources, thereby making Kazakhstan strong allies of immense strategic importance. Kazakhstan's support at the nuclear suppliers group during Indo-US Nuclear Deal negotiations were of immense importance to India.

Kazakhstan has 3.3 percent of the world's proven oil reserves and 1.7 percent of gas reserves. Its combined onshore and offshore proven hydrocarbon reserves have been estimated between 9 and 40 billion barrels. Kazakhstan's petroleum industry accounts for roughly 30 percent of the country's GDP and over half of its exports[24].

Kazakhstan has gas reserves of approximately 70 trillion cubic ft. There are plans to increase its annual gas output to nearly 2.3 trillion cubic ft. by 2016.[25] Karachaganak natural gas and condensate field is the largest source of natural gas in the country. Kazakhstan has Central Asia's largest recoverable coal reserves. Efforts are being made to increase coal production further. An investment of $500 million by Arcelor – Mittal to increase coal production in the Karaganda region is a step in this direction.[26] Kazakhstan is emerging as a major transit route for gas from Turkmenistan to Russia and other markets.[27] Though geopolitical maneuvering by different player in the region such as USA, EU, China and Iran to have greater access to Kazakhstan oil has started long back. India due to its late entry has missed many good opportunities, but has been working seriously to enter into the energy sector of the region with full dedication.

Kazakhstan has 1.5 million tons of uranium deposits, constituting approximately 17 per cent of the world total. These are the second largest deposits of uranium in the world. Kazakhstan is planning to increase uranium production from the current 6,673 metric tons uranium (MTU) to 30,000 tons MTU by the end of 2018. It is expected that with this new expansion plan, KazatomProm, the nodal national atomic company has plans to increase the share of uranium supply from the present 12 per cent to 30 per cent of total world uranium output by 2016.[28]Energy companies in Kazakhstan is promoting joint ventures to increase prospective shares in various segments of uranium market viz 12 per cent of uranium conversion market, 6 per cent of enrichment, and 30 per cent of the fuel fabrication market.[29]Kazakhstan and India have signed five important agreements/MoUs. MOU includes cooperation in civil nuclear energy and in hydrocarbons sector.[30]These agreements have catapulted Kazakhstan and India's relations to a higher strategic level.

It has been agreed that NPCIL (Nuclear Power Corporation of India) will annually import 120 tons of uranium from Kazakhstan under the nuclear agreement signed between India and Kazakhstan for supply of uranium to India for civilian nuclear energy programme. Technical cooperation with Kazakhstan has taken place in relation to fuel cycle developments, nuclear reactor construction and uranium fuel assemblies.[31]Various joint ventures in this sector took place between India and Kazakhstan like the Kazakh Uranium mining joint venture, Indo-Kazakhstan Uranium Resources Investment Company, joint venture on rare earth metals, Power Corp of India (NCPI) and KazAtomProm joint development and marketing initiative in innovative small and medium-sized nuclear reactors.[32]

India and Kazakhstan have signed hydrocarbon agreements raising the stake of ONGC Videsh Ltd. (OVL) and its partner Mittal Energy Limited's (OMEL) in Satpayev oil field from 10 per cent to 25 per cent with an investment of about US$ 400 million. The 1,582 sq km Satpayev block, situated in the Caspian Basin of Kazakhstan hold up to 253 million tons of recoverable deposits, which is equivalent to 1.85 billion barrels of oil.[33]Regional conflicts and major power rivalry are the biggest impediments in the growth of inter and intra-regional energy trade in Eurasia. Shortest routes from Kazakhstan to India pass through Afghanistan, Pakistan and Iran. Iranian route is one of the most economical routes for transportation of oil to India. The route that could connect Kashagan and Tengiz oil fields in Kazakhstan via eastern Caspian shore, through Turkmenistan to Iranian border is viable route. From here, a pipeline could pass across eastern Iran to the Persian Gulf terminal of Bandar Abbas in Persian Gulf.[34]

Few Indian and Kazakh energy experts proposed that another Pipeline could pass through Almaty, Korgas, Yinning, Kuqa, Aksu, Kashgar, Yarkand, Yecheng along the Xinjiang-Tibet Highway

(No. 219) Mazar, Shahidulla, Sumxi, Derub, Resum, Shiquanhe, Gar, Kailash, Burang and Lepu-Lekh in India. (Lipu-Lekh pass in Uttarakhand (India), has been already opened for border trade between India and China since 1992). The total distance of this route would be less than 3,000 kilometers as compared to the over 5,000 kilometers via Iran.[35]Nonetheless, if India and China agrees on this route, then this can have immense economic benefits for all the three countries. The short term option for oil trade between India and Kazakhstan at present is the swamp deals through Iranian, CPC and BTC pipelines systems, till the new shorter direct oil transit routes between India and Kazakhstan materializes.

Another significant energy reach country of the region is Azerbaijan. In fact medieval travelers have written about Azerbaijan's abundant supply of oil since the 9th century. Referred to as the oil capital of the region, Azerbaijan drilled its first oil well in 1846 in Bibi Heyat near Baku. After the break-up of the Soviet Union in 1991, there was only one route that carried its energy northwards to Russia. Azerbaijan was dependent on Russia for transporting its oil to other markets. Therefore, Azerbaijan was keen to diversify its export pipeline infrastructure. In the year 2006 its first export pipeline the Baku-Tbilisi-Ceyhan (BTC) became operational. This pipeline offered an opportunity to reach out to Western markets bypassing Russia.[36]Azerbaijan's position as a hub of export pipeline infrastructure was further augmented when Kazakhstan joined the BTC in 2008.[37]

India's energy cooperation with Azerbaijan gathered momentum only in late 1990's. For India access to Azerbaijan is not easy because of its landlocked status. Moreover, in the early years of its independence, Azerbaijan focused on constructing its export pipeline to the Western markets. However, gradually things began to change. It was the operationalization of the BTC that opened up opportunities for India to access Azerbaijan's energy resources as well as that of the Caspian Sea region. The Joint Working Group (JWG) between India and Azerbaijan also has been set up to promote the energy cooperation.

There is an excellent prospect for India to acquire Azerbaijani oil via the Turkish port of Ceyhan. Incidentally, India has already procured Azerbaijani oil worth US $ 2.4 billion. However, such an arrangement needs to be institutionalized. The possibility of extending the Ashkelon- Eilat pipeline system to India is not difficult to envisage. Azerbaijani oil could be brought via tankers from Ceyhan to Ashkelon in Israel on the Mediterranean Sea. This oil further could be fed into the Ashkelon–Eilat pipeline which brings it to Eilat in Israel on the Gulf of Aqaba. From Eilat tankers could bring Azerbaijani oil to Mumbai via tankers. The advantage of this route is that it could avoid the Suez Canal which is highly congested.[38]

This route could reduce the time taken for oil tankers to reach India from around 40 days to 19 days. This could be a viable proposition and needs to be given consideration at the highest level, more so when world attention is already focused on Azerbaijan's energy. Other ways of acquiring Azerbaijani oil through swap deals, (these could take place via Iran. Earlier India acquired Kazakh oil in this manner). Such a possibility could be explored too.[39] Thus, for India it is important to be visible on the energy market of Azerbaijan in the Caucasus region. This could prove advantageous for India in the long run.

Conclusion

Today, the geopolitical realities are to take, bold, innovative and visionary approaches in inter-state relations, including in the area of energy security. Eurasian energy project as mentioned requires a conceptual breakthrough in current geopolitical thinking among decision-makers in key countries around the world. If this happens, there would be favourable long-term consequences for the whole world. The Eurasian region could be transformed into a energy hub uniting major Eurasian energy producers, consumers and transit countries in a web of inter-dependence. Eurasian region could be transformed into a strategic space uniting major Eurasian energy producers including consumers and transit countries in a web of interdependence. Eurasian region could become the crossroads of a 21st century 'Silk Route', with gas and oil pipelines replacing caravan convoys. This whole region could become a zone of peace and development, through cooperation and partnership rather than of confrontation and conflict.

The joint ventures and collaboration could also act as a huge stimulus for the global economy. These would not only bring all-round economic advantage, prosperity, social and political stability, but also create a solid and enduring foundation for greater trust, confidence and understanding, extensive people-to-people ties and communication links that could lead to new lasting and stale political and strategic relationships between the countries of the region.

Given geo-strategic location and size, India's growing economic and military strength and its position as a significant consumer of energy, India will be very much a part of global energy geopolitics often key determinants of many bilateral relationships and invariably have a regional even a global, significance. India and the Eurasian States jointly need to give much greater and more focused attention to security concerns, energy issues and on the development strategies in its foreign energy and security policies. Energy security considerations need to be fitted into existing paradigms of foreign policy dynamics As India is aspiring to play an increasingly central role on the world stage; it has to evolve a determined, coordinated and sustained long-term strategy to ensure its energy security. India needs to develop a holistic energy policy that meshes into an overall strategy covering domestic policies and reforms, national security, economic development and environmental concerns. However, there is a need to formulate strategy and develop the necessary technicalities and put in place policies that will address India's security concerns in the coming decades.

End Notes

1 http://www.silkroadstudies.org/new/inside/publications/0505 Conference_Total.pdf.

2 http://www.realinstitutoelcano.org/wps/portal/rielcano_eng/ Content?WCM_GLOBAL_CONTEXT=/elcano/elcano_in/zonas_ in/dt59-2009.

3 *Central Eurasian Studies Review*, available at http://www.cesr-cess. org/CESR_contribution.html accessed on 16th February 2011.

4 see Sikri Rajeev, Challenge & Strategy, Sage, India, 2009.

5 Gusenov Rauf, 'Russian Energy Companies in Central Asia', *Central Asia and the Caucasus*, No.29, 2004, pp. 60-69.

6 Rudger Ahrend, 'Russia's Post-Crisis Growth: Its Sources and Prospects for Continuation', *Europe Asia Studies*, Vol.58, (1), January 2006, pp. 1-14.

7 Anders Ausland, 'The Hunt For', *Foreign Policy*, 152, Jan.Feb.2006, pp.43-48.

8 Gidadhubli RG. India's Economic Relations with Russia: Performance and Potentialities. In Dash. AlsoSee India will demand stake in Sakhalin, Times of India, January 25, 2007.

9 P.L. Dash., 'Russia: The Demographic Danger', in Jha Shashikant and Sarkar Bahaswati, (eds). *Amidst Turbulence and Hope, Transition in Russia and Eastern Europe,* Lancer, New Delhi, pp345-347.

10 see Rudger Ahrend, Russia's Post-Crisis Growth: Its Sources and Prospects for Continuation, *Europe Asia Studies*, Vol.58, No.1, January 2006, pp. 1-14.

11 See, *Tatneft Returns to the Middle Eastern States*, Tatneft Press Report, September 14, 2005, Also see *Budget for the First Nine Months of 2005*, in Tatneft's Review Report, November 30, 2005; Also see Tatneft Research Report on *Tatneft's Geological Research in Syria*, January 17, 2006.

12 Grigpty,Gritsenko *Presidential Discount*, available at http://www. polit.ru.

13 See Vladimir Milov, 'Global Energy Agenda', Russia in Global Affairs, Vol.3, (4) Oct-Dec.2005,pp. 60-68

14 Amb.Rajeev Sikri's speech on 12th November at the Eurasia-India Conference in New Delhi

15 Joshi Nirmala, "India's Energy cooperation with Azerbaijan", in Kundu Das Nivedita Ed. *India-Azerbaijan: the Silk Route Connections*, Academic Foundation, Delhi 2012,pp59-61

16 Harsh Pant, *India in a Multi Polar World*, 2007

17 Gael Raballand, Esen Ferhat, 'Economics and Politics of Cross border Oil Pipelines', Asia Europe Journal, Vol.5, (1), March 2007,pp.133-146.

18 Kazi Aftab Is the Proposed Russia-China-India Pipeline Feasible? Available at http://www.cacianalyst.org/newsite/?q=node/549 accessed on 19th june2007.

19 See Arbatov Alexander, Vladimir Feygin, Victor Smirrov, 'Unrelenting Oil Addiction', Russia in Global Affairs, Vol.3, (2) April-Jun 2005,pp.142-157.

20 See Sergy Tolstov, "Energy Security in the Interrelations among the EU, RF, Ukraine and Central Asia, Central Asia and the Caucasus, No.42, 2007, pp. 7-18.

21 http://www.kremlin.ru/appears/2006/02/13/1653_type63378 type63381_101609.shtml. accessed on April10, 2007

22 This agreement was signed during the visit of a high-profile delegation led by Tatarstan's President Rustam Minnikhanov to Jamnagar Gujarat (India) on March 2012

23 See http://www.sakhalin1.com/index.asp. Also See Ausland Anders, The Hunt For, in *Foreign Policy*, 152, Jan.Feb.2006, pp.43-48

24 Sullivan Stephen O., 'Russia: Pipeline Politics', Petroleum Economist, Vol.70, (11) Nov. 2003, pp. 26-27.

25 See Kundu Das Nivedita, Russia, 'Energy Supplier to the World?', *Indian Express*, New Delhi, December 20 ,2006, p20.

26 Kundu Das Nivedita., 'Russia and the Former Soviet States: Dynamics

of Relations', *Policy Perspective*, Vol. 4, (1), Jan-Jul 2007, Islamabad, Pakistan, pp.49, 59.

27 Pabst, Adrian, *Central Eurasia in the Emerging Global Balance of Power*, American foreign Policy Interest, Volume 31, Number 3, May 2009, pp. 166-176.

28 Mohanty Deba, Russian Aviation Industry Trends, *Air Power*, Vol.21, No.1, Spring 2005,pp. 91-103. Also See *SIPRI Year Book*, 2006, pp. 446-448.

29 Hanks Reuel R. *Global Security watch-Central Asia*, 2010.

30 Feygin Vladimir, 'Are the Energy Majors in Decline', *Russia in Global Affairs*, Vol. 5, (1), Jan-March 2007,pp25-51.

31 Naira Mkrtchyan, "Armenians in India and Indians in Armenia,"in S. Paramjit Sahai (ed.), *India-Eurasia: The Way Ahead*, Chandigarh: CRRID, 2008, pp.203-205.

32 *Rossiya kak Energeticheskaya Sverkhderzhava'*, IMEMO Press Release no. 386, February 1, Moscow, 2006,pp.1-27.

33 Naira Shovgaryan, "Cultural Links between Armenia and India", in S. Paramjit Sahai (ed.), *India-Eurasia: The Way Ahead*, Chandigarh: CRRID, 2008, pp.258-260

34 Daily News Analyses, "Government approves signing pact for TAPI gas pipeline project", December 11, 2010.

35 IMEMO, Research Report on *Rossiya kak Ekonomicheskaya Sverkhderzhava*, Moscow, March 2006.

36 Reports Published in the *Izvestia* and *Ria Nosvosti*, July 2006.

37 Economic Intelligence Unit, London, Country Report, Azerbaijan, February 2009.

38 Joshi Nirmala, "India's Energy cooperation with Azerbaijan", in Kundu Das Nivedita Ed. *India-Azerbaijan: the Silk Route Connections*, Academic Foundation, Delhi 2012, pp59-61.

39 ibid.

Reference

BP's Statistical Review of World Energy 2008.

International Energy Outlook 2009, DOE/EIA.

Shahram Akbarzadeh, *Uzbekistan and the United States*, Palgrave Macmillan, New York, 2005,pp1-7.

Yekaterina Kuznetsova, "The Near Abroad: Increasingly far away from Russia", Russia in Global Affairs, Vol.3, No.1, January-March, 2005, p.27.

Bolshaia Sovetskaia Entsiklopedia, Moscow: Sovetskaia Entsiklopediia, 1977, p.255.

Nacelenia Rossia, Edzegodniyie Demographicheskie Doklad, Center Demographicheskie Chelavieka, Moscow, 1993, pp 15-20.

Tomohiko Uyama, ed. *Empire, Islam and Politics in Central Eurasia*, Slavic Eurasian Studies, No. 14. Sapporo, Hokkaido University, 2007, 376 pp.

Nationalism and Ethnic Conflicts in Transcaucasia in Comparative Perspective,"www.geocities.com. also see Zurab Davitashvilki, "The Ethno Political Situation in the Caucasus and the Problem of Oil in Transportation", http://ourworld.compuseve.com.

Sengupta Kim, Afhganistan:Russia steps in to help NATO, in The Independent World News, 27th October 2010.

Tabata Shinichiro (ed.), *Dependent on Oil and Gas: Russia's Integration in to the World Economy*, Osamu Ieda, Japan, 2006,pp. 1-7. Also see Thane Gustabfson, *Crisis amid Plenty: The Politics of Soviet.*

Energy under Brezhnev and Gorbachov. Princeton, 1992.

Marshall Goldman, *The Enigma of Soviet Petroleum: Half Empty or Half Full?* London: George Allen & Unwin, 1980, pp.163–64.

Lane David, (ed.), *The Political Economy of Russian Oil*, Lanham MA & Oxford:Rowman & Littlefield.

BP Statistical Review of World Energy (Oil) July 2005.

'Russian Oil 2005: Rising Red Star', Report of United Financial Group,

Moscow, April 7, 2006.

Kenneth Christopher, Russia Savors its New Market-Economy Status, *The Russian Journal,* Jun 17, 2002, available at *http://www.russoft. org/docs/?doc=643.*

Gusev Leonid, '*Russia-Kazakh Cooperation in the Sphere of Energy*', paper presented in the international seminar on Energy and Transport Linkages between Central Asia and South Asia, on November 25th 2006, Indian Council for the Social Science Research, New Delhi, India.

Letche M. John, 'Russia Moves into the Global Economy', London, Routledge, 2007, pp35-43.

Stulberg Adam , 'Moving Beyond the Great Game', *Geopolitics,* Vol.10 (1), 2005,pp1-25.

Nakamur Yasushi, *Extractive Industries and 'Dutch Disease*', Discussion Paper, 99/5, Department of Economics, Heriot-Watt University, 1999.

Statistical data of Ministry of Industry & Energy of Russian Federation, May 2001.

4

Network Diplomacy and the Rise of New Regional Organisations

With the advent of the new century, the international environment in which India and the Eurasian states play the part of sovereign actors has become more intricate and complicated. The commonality of the key national interests and good economic relations creates possibility for cooperation between these great economic powers.

There are many issues on which India and the Eurasian States can cooperate and coordinate despite many asymmetries. Comprehensive cooperation between India and the Eurasian states are the suitable option in the present global scenario. There are many similarities in the socio-economic conditions between these states. Face to face with the globalisation, the problems they are encountering today also have commonalities. India's cooperation with the Eurasian states has great importance in terms of geopolitics. Undoubtedly, India and the states of Eurasia have great human resources and huge market potential. Many multilateral organizations like SCO (Shanghai Cooperation Organisation), BRICS (Brazil-Russia-India-China),RIC (Russia-India-China), CICA (Conference on Interaction and Confidence Building Measures in Asia), CAREC (Central Asian Regional Economic

Cooperation), EurAsEC (Eurasian Economic Community), Customs Union, Eurasian Union are growing in the region and it is expected that the relationship would grow further and these multilateral oragnisations will help in expanding the network and regional cooperation to a new height.

Shanghai Cooperation Organisation (SCO)

One of the significant multilateral organisations that have developed in the region is the SCO. The SCO is an inter-governmental international organization founded in Shanghai on 15 June 2001, by six countries: China, Russia, Kazakhstan, Kyrgyzstan, Tajikistan and Uzbekistan. These six countries are the member states of SCO and amongst them Russia and China are the main pillars of the SCO. These member states cover an area of over 30 million square km or about three fifths of Eurasia, with a population of 1.5 billion, about a quarter of the world's total. Its working languages are Russian and Chinese. India, Pakistan, Mongolia, Iran and Afghanistan are the Observer States of SCO. Belarus, Srilanka, Turkey are the Dialogue Partners.

The SCO's charter, adopted in 2002, states that the main purpose of SCO is to strengthen mutual trust, good-neighbourliness and friendship among members as well as observer states; develop effective co-operation in political affairs, economy, trade, science and technology, culture, education, energy, transport, environmental protection, maintaining regional peace, security and stability.

Evolution and Institutions of SCO

The SCO charter defines that the SCO forum should respect each other's independence, sovereignty and territorial integrity; non-interference in each other's internal affairs and not to use any force against each other and that settlement of any issues should be done through consultations. The SCO has become a significant forum for addressing politico-security and economic issues and concerns of the region The SCO through collective efforts is responding to the threats of terrorism, armed conflict and instability in the region.

Presently, the organization prioritizes on peace and security issues and also deals with issues of terrorism and separatism and focuses on making the whole region stable and peaceful.[1] Over the past few years SCO has emerged as the most influential multilateral institution in the region; SCO has become significant forum for addressing political, security as well as economic issues and concerns.

The SCO's economic agenda and cooperation between the member states has developed significantly. The economic cooperation is further gaining regional multilateral dimensions. The SCO has removed many obstacles for trade, now it is also working towards investment in the development projects particularly for building infrastructure such as roads and railways and has also simplified procedures for banking operations among member and observer states.[2] There are reports that trade has grown rapidly over the past few years between SCO member States as the economies of all the SCO member and observer states have grown reasonably.

SCO has adopted a programme of trade and economic co-operation, setting out some key economic objectives to be realised by 2020. SCO is also trying to create favourable conditions for the free movement of goods, capital, technology and services within the members as well as observer states. Even joint working groups have been set up for co-operation in electronic sectors, commerce and customs and for investment promotion. The SCO implemented more than 120 projects, including construction of roads and railways, joint telecom schemes for promoting cross-border trade etc.[3]

Transportation networks are crucial for regional economic cooperation. To connect China, Tajikistan, Pakistan and India with the rest of the Central Asian and Caspian region, new roads are being built. Efforts are also being made for improving north-south corridor and an energy grid corridor to link Russia with South Asia via Iran. Work is also in progress to improve air communications across the SCO region.[4]The UNDP (United Nations Development Programme) has contributed funds for the Silk Road Regional Programme under the UNDP-SCO partnership programme. Many new economic bodies including the SCO Banking Consortium have been developed for smooth economic cooperation. These banks help in developing closer links for settling various technical issues. The Consortium and the Business Council also helps in preparing joint investment programme for the SCO and for handling major infrastructure projects including energy, telecom, transport and cross-border trade.

Though SCO's economic agenda is wide, some ambiguity however exists in developing certain programmes and projects. China has been actively and consistently promoting the idea of a free-trade zone within the SCO. It is evident that the economic dimension of the SCO is set to expand further in the coming years. It is also expected that many new joint projects will be developed for providing energy security to the SCO members as well as to the observer states. The SCO has also set up a working group for developing energy and communication technology, hence, it is expected SCO members and observers can strengthen their economic relationship further as well as can also cooperate in addressing the security concerns of the region.

SCO and Regional Anti-Terrorist Structure (RATS)

One of the most important institutions of SCO after the secretariat is the Regional Anti-Terrorist Structure (RATS). This agency started its operation in the year 2004 from a base in Tashkent. Russian Federal Security Service (RFSB) is of the opinion that

RATS should also concentrate to fight against the latest threats of drug trafficking and cyber crimes along with exchange of information and co-ordination of operations related to tapping terrorist training camps and funding agencies. The RATS staffs include officials from all the SCO member states. Over the past few years, RATS has expanded its role. It is now working for the harmonisation of anti-terrorist legislation in the member-states and fight against the terrorist activities.[5] Through RATS, SCO is trying to find a common position to fight against various terrorist organisations within the region.

SCO in the Context of Eurasia

SCO has become an institution for confidence-building structure and through SCO Eurasian States have strengthened their relationship further, especially in the areas of security cooperation and energy policy coordination. Until recently, the SCO members addressed energy issues only bilaterally, but, in order to coordinate energy strategies and strengthen energy security, the organisation launched a energy club that unites energy-producing and energy-consuming states, including transit countries and private companies together.

SCO over the years became fully ready to take the challenges emanating from neighbouring Afghanistan. Most of the SCO member/observer states share common border with Afghanistan. Afghanistan's significance for the Central Asian SCO states like Tajikistan and Uzbekistan is immense as apart from sharing borders, they also share very close historical and cultural ties with the people of Afghanistan. The people of Northern Afghanistan are essentially of the same ethnic stock as Central Asian Uzbeks and Tajiks. Thus, the ethnic, social, cultural and political relationships between them are deep-rooted. Consequently, the two decades of crisis in Afghanistan had its repercussions on these countries too. It has been observed that in the more recent years, the Islamic Movement of Uzbekistan (IMU) was provided bases, training and access to the arms market by the Taliban. The IMU, with Taliban support carried out incursions into Uzbekistan and Kyrgyzstan. Further, refugees from the Afghan civil war in Tajikistan were influenced by developments in Afghanistan. Also, much of Afghanistan's drug production flows to Russia through Central Asia. All these factors make SCO to intervene into Afghanistan for maintaining peace and stability in the region. It is expected that this regional grouping like SCO could motivate certain groups inside Afghanistan to join internal conflict resolution talks. The members and observers of SCO can address the Afghans concerns jointly, as all SCO members and observers have vested interests in stabilizing situation in Afghanistan. Hence, it is possible that the SCO will assume responsibility on the issues related to the security concerns of the region very significantly.

SCO is trying to promote co-operation among its member and observer states in the sphere of security, politics, trade, economic, scientific-technical, as well as in energy and transportation spheres. Today, SCO has matured as an international organization and has expanded its influence.

Discourse on SCO

Scholars, policy makers and strategic community in Russia, China, India, Central Asia, Europe and USA vary significantly in their assessment of the SCO's functional outcomes for regional cooperation. While some credit the SCO with growing stability and predictability of regional situation[6] others consider this organization to be a mechanism of preserving authoritarian regimes in Central Asia.[7]

Discourse on Regional Cooperation within the SCO Framework

Russia has a diverse experience of cooperation with Central Asia during the previous two decades. Few Russian researchers however question the systemic nature of this experience noting that Central Asia does not represent a consolidated direction in Russian foreign policy making.[8]Rather the past decade has witnessed a diversification of Russia's partnerships in the region with a clear emphasis on the relationship with Kazakhstan. At the same time, various attempts to interact with Central Asian states under the frameworks of Commonwealth of Independent States[9], Common Security Treaty Organization[10], Central Asian Cooperation organization[11], and Eurasian Economic Cooperation organization became significant to create more or less viable mechanism of multilateral cooperation in the region.

Official Russian discourse singles out SCO as a special framework to carry out important decisions of Russian foreign policy. The recent Foreign Policy concept of Russia notes that the SCO should become a part of the Asia-Pacific network of regional cooperation mechanisms. Also mentions that the SCO along with the United Nation,(UN) Commonwealth of Independent States (CIS) and Collective Security Treaty Organisation (CSTO) should play a decisive role in stabilizing Afghanistan.[12] Indeed the SCO has the potential to enhance its role not only in the region but also in the global arena by playing a proactive role in stabilizing Afghanistan. Despite the fact that the SCO cannot ensure the full military integration of its members, the organization is an important political actor in the region.[13]In contrast to the official position, Russian research discourse on the SCO focuses on the following important features of the organization for Russian foreign policy.

The SCO has strategic importance for Russia. In this context, some Russian experts connect the strategic importance of the SCO with its function of additional security for Russian frontier, a supplement to CSTO[14] and an important regional framework to interact with Central Asian states. In this case CSTO and the SCO represented as complementary institutions, though the process of decision making within CSTO and the SCO differ significantly.

Many Russian experts emphasizes that the SCO as a regional Institution differs from European and American regional organizations[15]. They regard SCO as a regional or even trans-regional organization which provides assistance for the cooperation between the states with different models of political development and through this cooperation ensures the stability in Central Asia and in the neighboring States[16].This understanding differs from the approach to regional security cooperation based on the convergence of values.[17]

Some Russian experts credit the SCO for increasing cooperation in the energy and infrastructural sectors thus, creating the conditions for common economic and infrastructural space in Eurasia.[18]Political scientist Sergei Luzianin argues that to achieve SCO's aims and objectives the SCO should rely more on its cooperation with the observer states[19]. The importance of observer states for Russia in the SCO will rise because of the power in the region. Maintains close cooperative relationship with all other observer States. Thus, Russia wants to use SCO's diplomatic track to ensure the implementation of regional projects which correspond to Russian and interests, enable Russia to establish working ties with the observer states.

China's view of Regional Cooperation within the SCO Framework

For quite a long period China was not an active participant of the multilateral regional cooperation projects. However, on the bilateral level China started to restore inter-regional trade and cultural ties between its border regions and Central Asian republics in 1980s when on one hand, Sino-Soviet relations entered the phase of normalization and on the other hand, the reforms proclaimed by Den Xiaoping required a more intensified trade and economic relationship with the outside world. After the collapse of the Soviet Union, China established diplomatic ties with all Central Asian states in 1992.

National security issues and economic aspects define China's contemporary foreign policy aims in Central Asia. Geographically the region is linked to Xinjiang-Uighur autonomous region, one of China's most turbulent areas populated by the ethnic groups of Turkic origin. Central Asia's energy resources determine the region's economic significance for China's foreign policy.

Currently, as opposed to the state of Russia's relations with Central Asia, one can speak of China's consolidated strategy towards the region alongside with bilateral level of relations. This strategy has security and economic dimensions preconditioned due to reasons stated above. Within these dimensions Zhao Huasheng a strategic analysts named several priorities of China's strategy in the region, including the battle against terrorism, extremism and separatism, security of border areas, regional stability, China's participation in the economic development of Central Asia and access to the regional energy resources. According to the Chinese Scholars, China should not let any anti-Chinese state or military block get the dominating positions in the region.[20]

China's engagement in the Shanghai process in the late 1990s and further in the SCO activities added one more priority, namely strengthening of China's positions in this multilateral organization. China started to shape the so-called 'belt of good neighborhood' alongside the perimeter of its borders. Moreover, during 1990s, China was much more proactive in Central Asia than in East Asia trying to avoid the 'second front' of competition with the US.

Chinese experts view the SCO as an institutional framework where China can test the model of the multilateral leadership with China itself being one of the leading states. [21]According to the Director of Shanghai Cooperation Organization Studies Center in Shanghai, Pan Gung, Chinese leadership in the SCO is based on three pillars.[22]The first pillar is the Shanghai spirit or the principles which frame the conceptual vision of the SCO development. The principles of the Shanghai spirit were formulated by the then President of the People's Republic of China Jiang Zemin in his speech during the SCO meeting. They include the mutual trust, mutual benefit, equality, respect to different civilizational backgrounds and mutual prosperity.[23]Other two significant points mentioned by the Chinese leadership include the support to the SCO to further institutionalize the organisaion and support SCO's multilateral projects[24].

Central Asian States' view of Regional Cooperation within the SCO Framework

The views on SCO in Kazakhstan, Uzbekistan, Kyrgyzstan and Tajikistan vary significantly.

Kazakhstan, being one of the most active proponents of Eurasianism as the basis for re-integration of the post-Soviet space in general supports all the viable forms of regional cooperation in Central Asia. However, Kazakhstan does not want to be bounded by Russian and Chinese leadership in the SCO perceiving itself as a "creative leader" in the region.[25]

Uzbekistan pursues more unilateral strategy in the region and traditionally has a negative attitude towards Central Asian integration or cooperation projects like SCO. It rather makes an emphasis on the bilateral relations with Russia and other partners, including US, trying to balance among them to maximize its own benefits. Uzbekistan tries to refrain from any collective, especially military activities under the frameworks of regional organizations, including the SCO.[26]However, the SCO itself still remains as one of the regional institutional frameworks where Uzbekistan maintains its presence.

Kyrgyzstan and Tajikistan are quite depended on SCO mechanisms in terms of ensuring their national security.[27]At the same time, the official discourse of Kyrgyzstan and Tajikistan stresses that the SCO is important not only as a multilateral structure per se but also as a mechanism of strengthening bilateral ties between the states.[28] For both countries, post-2014 Afghanistan presents a source of security concern which they cannot fully address by their own means.

For Central Asian states, especially Kyrgyzstan, Tajikistan and Uzbekistan, the SCO also serves as a platform for discussion on energy, water, railroad connection etc. which are unlikely to be resolved bilaterally.[29]

India's view of Regional Cooperation within the SCO Framework

India's current foreign policy is aimed at achieving and sustaining the status of not only regional leader in South Asia, but also a pan-Asian player.[30] Indian political elite regards a broader cooperation with Central Asia and India's greater presence in the Eurasian region is considered as a logical step in obtaining the status of Asia's leading actor.[31] The research discourse among the strategic community regards Eurasia as a region of new strategic neighborhood.[32] For India its interaction with the SCO is important as an element of its cooperation with the States of the Eurasian region.[33]

European and American views of the SCO

There are several interpretations of the SCO activities in the European and American research discourse. The dominating trend is to regard SCO as the geopolitical balance-of-power and a policy forum. The extreme version of this geopolitical approach also stresses the SCO's role in preserving and legitimizing authoritarian political regimes in the region. This approach views either the SCO or its relationship with the observer states (first and foremost Iran) as directed against the West and the US.[34] Meanwhile some researchers view the SCO as an instrument which China and Russia use to preserve their regional dominance in Central Asia. While Russia took the responsibility to develop military and political cooperation, China enjoys the dominant position in the economic cooperation with the region. Thus, the two countries maintain their leading status in Central Asia through SCO.[35]However, a more balanced approach views the SCO as an organization with a highly focused agenda aimed at solving region's internal problems and combating new threats[36].

European and American researchers usually stress the normative aspects of the SCO activities linking them with the problems of democratizing political regimes in the region. Emphasizing the SCO's ineffectiveness as an independent player, some experts note that the SCO needs external partnerships to sustain its activities, while its member states should undergo internal political changes too. For Russia and China the SCO is important not as a means of regional integration but as an instrument to structure the regional space without external involvement.

Russia-India-China (RIC)

Russia, India and China (RIC) have been interacting trilaterally since 1996. The main aim of this forum is to maintain international balance of power in favour of world peace. RIC's main agenda has been to oppose unilateralism. RIC believes that the diverse threats and risks cannot be addressed by military power alone but need to be appraised through political, social and economic prisms.

Russia-India-China's possible axis formation is an important political idea in the post-Cold War period advocated by President Yeltsin in 1993 and Prime Minister Primakov in 1996. RIC can stimulate the process of multi-polarism which will be of far reaching significance for international relations. Countries like Russia, India and China need a multi-polar world in order to get their national interest across and have autonomy of decision-making. To construct a multipolar world, the Russia-India-China triangle would be indispensable inspite certain unresolved issues between these countries. Movement between these three states towards a better understanding is evident. Russia-India relations flourished during the cold war period. Even after the end of cold war, the relationship was maintained as Russia proved to be India's trusted friend. Similarly, China-India relationship became smoother in the eighties and after the 1993 accord the economic relations were taken forward. Since then, there are continuous efforts to maintain the relationship on both sides. Russia-China relations have also taken a new shape after the end of cold war. Russia, China and India have a number of converging interests that could add substance to trilateral cooperation. All three states back the primacy of the United Nations in solving crises and support the principle of non-intervention in internal affairs of sovereign states. [37]In the long term, it is the mutual confidence which will help these three powers to play a larger role in global politics.

Prospects of relations between the three countries in the twenty-first century certainly imply coordinated actions taken in response to the challenges of the new century. There are many issues on which Russia, India and China can cooperate. All of them are committed to build a just and fair new international political and economic order. There are advantages in three-nation's cooperation despite the obvious asymmetries, given the fact that they are amongst the world's largest continental-sized entities. The agenda for future cooperation between China, India and Russia is extensive. Any discussion or reflection on the prospects and possibilities of cooperation between India, China and Russia began with the understanding of the wider context in which such cooperation would be possible and would progress.

All three countries have a long history of interaction, exchange, cooperation and close relationships. In the post-World War II period, there have been phases of tremendous warmth and dizzying highs among them. There have also been periods of near-total breakdown and actual hostilities.[38] However, what has become clear to all three is that any restructuring of relations would be based on a qualitatively different strategic reality that would be shaped by and impinged upon by the weight of history and would in some respects have to virtually start from scratch. This cooperation instead of affecting the independent foreign policies in negative way rather would help in strengthen the foreign policies of these Nations.

One of the major areas of cooperation for these three countries is in the energy sphere. Russia is an energy surplus country, whereas, China and India are energy deficient. Hence, these three states together could invest in joint projects that could facilitate the flow of oil and gas from Russia into China and India. All three countries of RIC Forum prevails multi-nationality. Due to historical reasons, there has been ethnic estrangement to different degrees leading to separatist movements. With each other's cooperation and through exchange of experiences ethnic problems can be solved and separatist activities in the region can also be curbed. Comprehensive Russia-India-China cooperation is the suitable option in the present Global scenario.

Indeed, the goal of trilateral cooperation is mutual benefit and most likely will conform to the interest of each country. The prospects of cooperation in technology, energy, raw material etc. are extremely broad. Important aspect of the tripartite cooperation is that its success is also subject to the social orientation. The population of each country should recognize the benefits of Russia-India-China cooperation so that it could gain massive support and could be deepened and widened further. Globalisation offers new opportunities and brings new challenges to China, India and Russia. In order to realize the opportunities and to respond to challenges, there is a need for permanent mechanism for exchange of views and coordination of actions.

Russia-India-China cooperation has great importance in terms of geopolitics. The population of these three countries together amounts to around 2.4 billion. They cover a total area of 29.96 million square kilometers which is 22.5 per cent of the total area of the world. Undoubtedly, the three countries have great human resources, huge potential of market and rich endowment of natural resources.

All the three countries, Russia, India and China are faced with the task of developing their economies. Of the three countries, China, Russia and India, China has common borders with both Russia and India. All three countries advocate non-alliance and non-confrontation. The relationship among the three countries affects the basic principles of Asian security. It will definitely have a positive impact on Asian security if their ties could be further improved. Thus, the prospects for the formation of Russia, India and China strong triangle is indeed very bright.

The three countries Russia-India-China have taken similar positions on many international political issues and concerns. All the three Countries are supportive of UN peace initiative. The RIC joint statement also reiterated their concerns on Afghanistan and emphasized on maintaining peace and security in and around Afghanistan.[39] RIC joint statements mentioned about their commitment to ensure stability in Afghanistan and reaffirmed their commitment to contribute towards ensuring stability and security within the UN framework or through other regional initiatives. The growing closeness amongst RIC is clearly noticeable in various forums, from the United Nations to the G-20 Summits, within SCO, during the Asia-Europe Meetings, during Climate Change meetings, during East Asian Summits and so on. RIC reflected collective stand in these Forums. Perhaps there is some difference in opinion on certain issues, but there is a certain sense that all three countries are favorable to the concept of a more plural, more democratic international order and that the three countries together can play an important role in bringing this together.

There are strong complementarities among the three countries, in terms of natural resources, services capability, skilled labour, manufacturing capability, technology and all three are strong on entrepreneurial activity and in innovation and technological activity. However, the current levels of trade, investment and economic interaction between them are far below their potential. There is a considerable scope for cooperating on technology and innovation making use of growth prospects for the three countries. RIC have already set up subsidiaries like RIC trilateral experts meeting on disaster management, trilateral business forum, and trilateral academic scholar's dialogue and conducted trilateral projects and conferences in these specialised fields.[40]Nonetheless, the idea of trilateral cooperation will need a greater push to come-up on the radar of the main stream decision making multi-lateral forum.

The regular meetings of the three countries foreign ministers takes place regularly for promoting the trilateral cooperation. The main task of the RIC forum is to create friendly relationship among the three countries and to improve the security paradigm in the region and also to strengthen mutual understanding and trust which is essential for finding the best solutions for certain problems at the bilateral level. The principles laid down in the trilateral dialogues are on the principles of equality, mutual trust and consensus. Trilateral cooperation has gained strong momentum and as long as patience and perseverance is maintained, cooperation of the three countries will develop further.

Brazil-Russia- India- China-South Africa (BRICS)

Another major organistion that is developing in the recent period is BRICS. BRICS is a grouping acronym that refers to the countries of Brazil, Russia, India, China and South Africa, where, all seemed to be at a similar stage of newly advanced economic development. BRICS contains roughly a third of the world's population and a fifth of its GDP. Today, trade among BRICS rose from $27 billion in 2002 to $ 212 billion in 2010, however, it is expected to reach $250 billion by 2013. It is expected that BRICS will be responsible for 56% of world's growth by 2014.[41] The World needs better economic structures and BRICS has come into widespread use as a symbol of the shift in global economic power away from the developed economies toward the developing world. It is expected that the economic potential of Brazil, Russia, India, China and South Africa is such that they could become among the five most dominant economies by the year 2050. Today BRICS is one of the biggest economic weights. They are the largest economies outside the OECD (Organisation for Economic Co-operation and Development). BRICS size, power and the growing global influence of its members have made it more attractive.

BRICS is considered as a serious transnational group that can play a key role in reforming the economic system and can contribute towards maintaining economic growth, peace and security. BRICS demonstrates how geographically distant countries with different social and economic challenges can become partners and generate a convergence that changes the axis of international politics. BRICS wants to take this cooperation forward on the basis of openness, solidarity, mutual understanding and trust and for promoting peace, security and development in a multi-polar, inter-dependent and increasingly complex globalizing world. BRICS wants to remain engaged with the world community to addresses the issues and the challenges for people's well-being and bring stability in a responsible and constructive manner.

Coordinating policy at the level of BRICS will not be easy, given that the political interests of BRICS members clash at various levels. Still, this group could be a channel for resolving many pressing global politico-economic concerns. BRICS Summits boost the momentum as it takes the BRICS agenda forward. The major themes are of better governance of the global economy and sustainable development or green economy issues. Moreover, the nature of the Bank is such that it would promote equal partnership with all countries as a way to deal with development issues.

BRICS also focused on formation of BRICS Institutions which would help cement five countries together a so-called formation of a "BRICS Bank," this could possibly fund development projects and infrastructure Bank. BRICS Banks idea is to make a powerful financial tool to improve trade opportunities. BRICS also agrees to play active part in the global fight against climate change and contribute to the global effort in dealing with climate change issues through sustainable and inclusive growth and not just by capping development.

BRICS acknowledge the relevance of Green Economy in the context of Sustainable Development and Poverty Eradication (GESDPE) as well as Institutional Framework for Sustainable Development (IFSD). BRICS is expanding sourcing of clean and renewable energy and use of energy efficient and alternative technologies. BRICS retreated that they will continue the efforts for the implementation of the Convention and its Protocols, with special attention to the Nagoya Protocol on accessing the Genetic Resources and the fair and equitable sharing of benefits arising from their utilization, Biodiversity Strategic Plan 2011-2020 and the Resource Mobilization Strategy.

BRICS co-operates intensively on a bilateral basis too. There have been joint military exercises conducted between Russia and China, Russia and India, and China and India in recent years. A benchmark equity index derivative shared by the stock exchanges of the five BRICS nations was also launched. The BRICS leaders are also expected to sign agreements allowing their individual development banks to extend credit to other members in local currency, a step towards replacing the dollar as the main unit of trade between them.

BRICS shares similar views on the International political situations too as BRICS expressed deep concern at the current situation in Syria and called for an immediate end to all violence and violations of human rights in that country. On Afghanistan, BRICS supports the global community's commitment to Afghanistan, enunciated at the Bonn International Conference on December 2011, to remain engaged over the transformation from 2015-2024. BRICS affirms the commitment to support Afghanistan's emergence as a peaceful, stable and democratic state, free of terrorism and extremism and underscore the need for more effective regional and international cooperation for stabilization including curbing terrorism. BRICS also extended support for combating illicit drug trafficking originating from Afghanistan within the framework of the Paris Pact.

Among BRICS countries there are nuclear powers as well as UN Security Council's permanent seat holders. BRICS has initiated various talks on strengthening the effort to cooperate and assist for reduction of natural disasters, for cooperation in the environmental protection sectors, cooperation in the business and commercial sectors, cooperation in the energy sector & cooperation in curbing terrorism. BRICS would be keen to strengthen friendship and partnership and work closely to ensure regional peace and stability and create a favourable condition for regional development. BRICS is also interested in promoting cooperation further and bring more benefits to the people of BRICS Nation.

One of the biggest obstacles that are expected to come on the way of BRICS development and growth is the environmental degradation causes. Another concern for BRICS is that substantial numbers of poor people are living in BRICS Nations, therefore, along with the economic growth, anti-poverty programs are also high up in their list of concerns which is becoming an obstacle for the rapid growth.[42]

BRICS has showed the new ways of international cooperation. There is a huge potential for the BRICS to cooperate in education sectors, in natural resources, in technological sectors, in agricultural sectors etc. Overall, BRICS aims to create a better world by promoting positive trends, by initiating deeper reform of the global economic governance system and greater cooperation to pursue a win-win situation for all BRICS nations. BRICS grouping also expects that these trends will be beneficial for developing more just and reasonable development of the international power politics and address security concerns in the region.

Conference on Interaction and Confidence Building Measures in Asia (CICA)

It is a well known fact that Asia has both a huge potential for development and a multitude of unresolved and potential conflicts that undermine its stability. Conference on Interaction and Confidence Building Measures in Asia (CICA) was convened by Asian states for enhancing cooperation towards promoting peace, security and stability in Asia. The idea of convening CICA was first proposed by President of the Republic of Kazakhstan Nursultan Nazarbayev on 5th October 1992, at the 47th Session of the United Nations General Assembly.[43] The moving spirit was the aspiration to set up an efficient multilateral structure for ensuring peace and security in Asia. Unlike other regions in the world, Asia did not have such a structure at that time and earlier attempts had not been very successful. But this initiative was supported by a number of Asian countries who felt that such a structure was the need of the time. One of the reasons for this support was the fact that CICA aimed to strengthen mutual understanding and create harmoniously designed security system on the Asian continent. CICA offered an opportunity to the Asian states not only for better understanding of each other's security concerns and to cooperate on monitoring and managing conflict issues, but also to help resolve many related problems through interaction in various sectors.

There were of course skeptics that the idea would not be workable because of the extreme diversity of the continent and existence of multiple flash points with significant conflict potentials. The skeptics have however, been proved wrong and today CICA is one of the diverse and ambitious groupings seeking mutually acceptable measures for resolving problem and conflicts in the region through dialogue and confidence building measures among the member states.

Continued relevance of CICA has been demonstrated by the fact that its membership has increased within last few years. CICA Member States account for nearly ninety percent of the area and population of Asia. CICA's reach extends from Turkey in the west to Republic of Korea in the east encompassing countries in Eurasia, Middle East, South, South East and East Asia.[44]This is perhaps the only platform outside of United Nations where countries, which even do not have diplomatic relations, come together for exchange of views on issues of common interest.

During the earlier years of its formation, member states worked hard to prepare an adequate legal basis. They prepared the declaration on the principles guiding relations between the CICA Member States adopted at the first Ministerial Meeting in 1999, the Almaty Act adopted at the first Summit Meeting in 2002 and the Catalogue of CICA Confidence Building Measures adopted during the Second Ministerial Meeting in 2004. These founding documents laid down the comprehensive approaches for addressing contemporary issues like conflict resolution, international terrorism, disarmament and arms control, confidence building measures, drug trafficking, illegal sale of fire-arms and nuclear materials, humanitarian issues including human trafficking, promotion of trade and well being of the people of the region.

From 2007 CICA has started the process of implementation of confidence building measures. Twelve member states are coordinating confidence building measures in wide range of issues including interaction in cultural, religious and educational affairs, tourism, development of small and medium enterprises, information technology, energy security, development of secure transport corridors, environment, disaster management, drug trafficking and on meeting new threats and challenges. CICA also wants to initiate deliberations on military-political issues which are vital for creating a common and indivisible area of security in Asia. Confidence building measures on military-political issues, which will help to understand each other's security concerns, to pave the way for stable political and diplomatic relations and most importantly, encourage moves to identify shared security needs.

Kazakhstan was the founding Chairman of CICA in the year 2002. There has been regular rotation every two years and a new member country becomes Chair of CICA to bring new dynamism and new ideas to the forum. CICA has made big strides in its endeavor to find ways and means to eliminate the causes of mistrust, tension and hostility and create conditions for sustainable peace in the region and economic growth of the Asian States. However, there is a need to do more. Today, no Nation can defend itself alone against contemporary threats and challenges.[45] Hence, Eurasia needs a comprehensive system of collective security. The challenge is to see whether there is a collective will to take concrete steps and rise to the occasion and if CICA can translate words and commitments into action.

Central Asia Regional Economic Cooperation (CAREC)

The CAREC programme, an initiative of the Asian Development Bank (ADB), was established in 1997 to promote economic cooperation amoung the countries of the Central Asian region. The CAREC member States are Afghanistan, Azerbaijan, China, Kazakhstan, Kyrgyzstan, Mongolia, Pakistan Tajikistan, Turkmenistan and Uzbekistan. In addition to ADB other multilateral Institutions involved in the project are European

Bank for Reconstruction and Development (EBRD), International Monetary Fund (IMF), Islamic Development Bank (IsDB), United National Development Programme (UNDP) and World Bank. CAREC also partners with other key regional groups like Shanghai Cooperation Organization (SCO) and the Eurasian Economic Community (EurAsEC). The prime focus of CAREC is for financing infrastructure projects and improving the region's transport and trade and energy policies. The aim of CAREC is mainly to improve regional economic cooperation.[46]

The member countries of the CAREC are meeting regularly and also ministerial Conferences are held regularly. In the 11th Ministerial Conference the CAREC Ministers group agreed to invest more than US$ 23 billion in building new regional transport infrastructure projects,[47] together with energy and trade initiatives to promote connectivity in the region.

Eurasian Economic Community (EurAsEC)

Eurasian Economic Community is an international organization that ensures multilateral economic cooperation among its member states. The Eurasian economic Community was founded according to the Treaty for the Establishment of the Eurasian Economic Community, signed by the presidents of the Republic of Belarus, the Republic of Kazakhstan, the Kyrgyz Republic, the Russian Federation and the Republic of Tajikistan, in Astana on October 10, 2000.[48]

In January 2006 the Republic of Uzbekistan joined the Community, but suspended its participation in the work of the EurAsEC's governing bodies since 2008. In May 2002, the Republics of Moldova and Ukraine were granted observer status at the EurAsEC and in April 2003 the same status was granted to the Republic of Armenia. In 2003, EurAsEC was granted observer status in the United Nations General Assembly (UN GA). During its 62nd session in December 2007 the UN GA adopted the resolution for "Cooperation between the United Nations and the Eurasian Economic Community (EurAsEC)".[49]

EurAsEC member states occupy a total area of 20.3 m sq. km. The trade turnover of the member states has increased three times since 2002 and in 2007 exceeded USD 90 bn. During the Inter-state Council meeting on August 16 2006 in Sochi heads of states like Alexander Lukashenko, Nursultan Nazarbayev, Kurmanbek Bakiyev, Vladimir Putin, Emomali Rakhmon and Islam Karimov made a decision to establish a customs union within the EurAsEC framework with the Republic of Belarus, the Republic of Kazakhstan and the Russian Federation as initial members. Other EurAsEC member states will join the customs union when their economies are ready to take this step. During the meeting on October 6, 2007 in Dushanbe, they considered the issue of forming the legal basis of the customs union and signed some agreements on the subject.[50]

The establishment of the EurAsEC customs union and common economic space will enable the Eurasian community to ensure effective use of existing economic potential to raise the living standard of its people.[51] A common economic space created by the Customs Union in January 2012, has opened a new chapter in the Eurasian economic regional integration process. Customs Union is a trade bloc consisting of free trade area, where member countries share a common external tariff and external trade policy. The main purpose behind the Customs Union is to boost economic cooperation and establish closer political and cultural ties among the member countries.

In June 2009, the Customs Union Members- Kazakhstan, Belarus and Russia agreed on a unified customs tariff. They also decided to establish a unified customs territory for a single market for goods, investment and labour. Citizens of the member states of the Union can travel within the member countries with an internal passport.

On 19th November 2011, the member states put together a joint commission on promoting closer economic ties and to create a Eurasian Union. President Nursultan Nazarbayev of Kazakhstan has proposed for the creation of a common currency to help countries address challenges like Global Economic Crisis. Number of Countries has expressed their willingness to join the group.

Eurasian Union

The Eurasian union is an economic and political Union, which evolved from the newly formed Customs Union in November 2011, the President of Belarus, Kazakhstan and Russia signed an agreement to create Eurasian Economic Union (EEU), which started from 2015 onwards. It aims to build on the existing Customs Union, which has removed trade barriers, facilitated free capital and labour movement among the three countries. Kyrgyzstan and Tajikistan are willing to join the Eurasian Union. In future, other post-Soviet Countries would be included. The organisation would aim at enhancing regional economic integration, including introduction of a single currency and deepening Eurasia's relationship with Europe and Asia.

The Primary regulating Institution is the Eurasian Economic Commission (EEC) launched in July 2012. It enforce rules and regulations and implement initiatives for further integration. This body is responsible for tariff and non-tariff regulations, regulating customs, monitoring and regulating macro-economics, economic competition, energy policy, financial policy, etc. It is also the permanent supranational governing body or regulatory agency of the EurasEC, common Economic Space and the Customs Union. Unlike the EU, the EEU commission will take decisions by majority vote and not by consensus.[52] Eurasian Union has got the potential to become one of the biggest common market in the world.

Conclusion

India and the Eurasian States are trying either to evade or minimize threats and challenge which are causing disastrous impacts in the region. This Chapter brings out the benefits and challenges for the regional cooperation through these organisations and network diplomacy. Today, Eurasian states are faced with various sorts of extremism manifesting within the region. The lingering and acute problem for India is also counter-terrorism, separatism and extremism. The world today is becoming ever more contradictory and unpredictable with the conflicts and growing uncertainties in international relations. Hence, India and the Eurasian states need to move towards a strategic vision for building the missing Asian architecture. India and the Eurasian countries of former Soviet States can work closely to use all existing and nascent regional initiatives such as SCO, BRICS, RIC, CICA, CAREC, EurAsEC, Customs Union, Eurasian Union etc. for strengthening cooperation with each other. India along with the Eurasian States can resolve the problems related to the arms control and the new threats and challenges on the nuclear front in a coherent manner. The regular meetings and interactions through these regional organisations are playing the key role at the moment in promoting the cooperation. It is also helping to strengthen the dialogue mechanism on the one hand and on the other hand to signal the readiness of the countries to counteract challenges and threats facing the region, to solve problems requiring close attention in the process of forming an adequate and harmonious world order.

India shares similar perceptions with the Eurasian States on how the international order should be looking like. India as well as Russia, Central Asian Republics and South Caucasus States of Eurasia have stressed the importance of multilateralism. All these countries are favorable to the concept of network diplomacy through regional organisations and forming plural, democratic international order. These countries all-together can play an important role in bringing innovative approach in solving complicated regional problems.

Today, the main focus of these forums and Organisations is to create cooperative, friendly relationship as well as to improve the whole politico-economic as well as security situation in the region through each other's cooperation and support. These forums can strengthen mutual understanding and trust which is essential for finding solutions for solving various regional issues and concerns and for maintaining peace and prosperity of the region.

Endnotes

1. Radyuhin Vladimir, *Russia for speeding up SCO expansion,* Hindu, 17ᵗʰ June, 2009.

2. Mark N. Katz, *SCO Regional Clout Bound to Increase,* Global Research, Voice of Russia, 7 September 2008.

3. *The Shanghai Cooperation Organisation,* available at http//www. sectsco.org.htmil.00039.html Also See http://www.bloomberg.com/ apps/news?pid=206 ", 01087&sid=arB8YCUjwaTY&refer=home.

4. Oresman M., *The SCO: A New Hope or to the Graveyard of Acronyms?* Available at http://www.csis.org.

5. Kundu Das Nivedita, *Sanghai Cooperation Organisation: Significance for India,* Indian Foreign Affairs Journal, Vol.4, No.3, July-September, 2009, pp.91-101.

6. Bailes at al. 2007.

7. Ambrosio 2008.

8. Malashenko 2012.

9. Nowadays CIS includes Russia, all Central Asian republics, Azerbaijan, Belorussia, Moldova and Ukraine.

10. CSTO includes Armenia, Belarus, Kazakhstan, Kyrgyzstan, Russia and Tajikistan. Uzbekistan has suspended its membership in 2012.

11. Central Asian Cooperation organization existed from the year 2002 up to 2005 with Kazakhstan, Kyrgyzstan, Tajikistan, Uzbekistan and Russia being members of it. In 2005 Central Asian Cooperation organization merged into Eurasian Economic Cooperation organization.

12. MFA of Russia, 2013.

13. Nikitina 2009.

14. Bailes et al. 2007, p. 44.

15. Nikitina 2011.

16. Bailes et al. 2007.

17. Adler and Barnett 1998.

18. Uyanov 2012, Lukin 2012.

19. Luzianin 2012.

20. Zhao, 2005.

21. Hunag Yunsong, 2014, Sichuan University Chengdu, China.

22. Pan Gung, 2008.

23. Jiang, 2001.

24. Nazarbayev, 2010.

25. Naumkin et al. 2013.

26. Russia's 201st Motorised Rifle Division protects Tajik -Afghan Border. Russia and Kyrgyzstan carry's out joint military trainings. The most recent military trainings "Dostuk-2013," took place in June 2013. They were aimed at combating potential terrorist threat and probable attacks on Kyrgyz Republic's border.

27. The use of this terminology becomes even more important if one takes into account that Taiwan, according mainland China, is also categorized as a separatist area.

28. http://www.Trend.az. 2012.

29. Aris, 2011, p71.

30. Kundu Nivedita 2012.

31. Voskressenski, 2010.

32. Sachdeva 2012.

33. Sachdeva, 2012, 80.

34. Cohen, 2006; Laruelle and Peyrouse 2012, 37.

35. Contessi 2010.

36. Aris 2011.

37. Ravi.N., "Russia-India-China: Trilateral Engagement", in *Russia-India-China: Evolution of Geopolitical Strategic Trends*, ed. Nivedita Das Kundu, Academic Foundation, New Delhi, 2010, pp 17-19.

38. Ibid.

39. Starr Frederick , A *'Greater Central Asia Partnership' for Afghanistan and its Neighbors,*Washington, D.C.:Central Asia-Caucasus Institute and Silk Road Studies Program, 2005.

40. Vardharajan Siddhath, "Six Propositions about the World Order and the Role of Russia-India-China", in *Russia-India-China: Evolution of Geopolitical Strategic Trends*, ed. Nivedita Das Kundu, Academic Foundation, New Delhi, 2010, pp 37-39.

41. KowittBeth,,*CNNMoney.com.http://money.cnn.com/2009/06/17/news/economy/goldman_sachs_jim_oneill_interview.fortune/index.htm.*

42. *Dreaming with BRICs,* Global Economics Paper No. 99, *How Solid Are the BRICs?*Global Economics Paper 134.

43. Trivedi Rmakant, 'Netradizionnye ugrozy bezopasnosti v Zentral'noy Azii s tochki zreniya stravnitel'noi regional'noi perspectivy [Nontraditional Security Threats in Central Asia in Comparative Regional Perspective]' *Sranitel'naya Politica [Comparative Politics],* No.4 (6), 2011, pp.109-123.

44. Ahamed Shri E. *Keynote Address by MOS Shri E. Ahamed at First India-Central Asia Dialogue.* June 12, 2012 Ministry of Foreign

Affairs of India URL: http://www.mea.gov.in/bilateral-documents. htm?dtl/19791/Keynote+address+by+MOS+Shri+E+Ahamed+at+ First+IndiaCentral+Asia+Dialogue (accessed April 6, 2013).

45. World Bank (2013) *World Development Indicators* URL: http://data. worldbank.org.

46. Country Reports: Central Asia, Institute for Economic Strategies, Central Asia, Almaty, Kazakhstan, January 2010.

47. UN (2013) *International Human Development Indicators* URL: http://hdrstats.undp.org/en/indicators/103106.html.

48. Richard A. Boucher, Assistant Secretary of State for South and Central Asian Affairs Statement to the House International Relations Committee Subcommittee on the Middle East and Central Asia '*U.S. Policy in Central Asia: Balancing Priorities (Part II)*' Washington, D.C., April 28, 2006 URL: http://commdocs.house.gov/committees/ intlrel/hfa27230.000/hfa27230_0f.htm (accessed July 22, 2013).

49. See http://www.evrazes.com/en/.

50. Sachdeva Gulshan, 'Central Asia. India's New Strategic Neighbourhood' *Geopolitics*, Vol.III, Iss.V, 2012, pp.79-81.

51. See www.chathamhouse.org.

52. Fioramonti Lorenzo, ed., *Regions and Crises. New Challenges for Contemporary Regionalisms*, Basingstoke: Palgrave Macmillan, 2012..

References

Mark N. Katz/Revolution: International Dimensions, CQ Press, 2001.

P. Stobdan, Stabilization: a view from India//. http://www.inosmi.ru/stories

Political processes in Kyrgyzstan 2008-2010/Political forecast.//the Center "the Policy Asia":

CIA World Factbook Data, available at https://www.cia.gov/library/publications/the-world-factbook/geos/af.html

Kuralay Baizakova, "Democratization and Political Stability in Kazakh-stan", *Himalayan and Central Asian Studies*, Vol. 10, No. 4, October-December 2006

Michal Camdessus, "Challenges facing Transition Economies of Central Asia", Address at the conference on challenges to Economies in Transition, Bishkek, 27 May 1998

"Central Asia: Country Risk Reports", Institute for Economic Strategies: Central Asia (Almaty: Kazakhstan, January 2009), p. 2.

ASEAN (2005) Memorandum of Understanding between the Secretariat of the Association of

Southeast Asian Nations (ASEAN Secretariat) and the Secretariat of the Shanghai Cooperation

Organization (SCO Secretariat). Available at: URL http://www.asean.org/ archive/ASEAN-SCO-MOU.pdf

IISS (2013) _e Military Balance. London: IISS. Eurasian Development Bank (2009) _e System of Indicators of Eurasian Integration. Almaty:

MFA of Russia (2013) 'Kontseptsiya vneshnei politiki Rossiyskoi Federatsii 12.02.2013' [_e Foreign

Policy Concept of the Russian Federation, February 12, 2013], Ministry of Foreign Affairs of Russia

Available at: URL http://www.mid.ru/brp_4.nsf/newsline/6D84DDEDE DBF7DA644257B160051BF7F

UN (2013) International Human Development Indicators. Available at: URL http://hdrstats.undp.org/ en/indicators/103106.html

World Bank Report, *From Disintegration to Reintegration: Europe and Central Asia in International Trade,*2006, available at http://www.worldbank.org/

United Nations Economic and Social Commissions for Asia and the Pacific, *"Transit Transport Issue in Landlocked and transit Developing*

Countries", Report No.ST/ESCAP/2270, 2003.

Ziyadov Taleh, "Azerbaijan as a regional hub in Central Eurasia", Azerbaijan Diplomatic Academy, Baku, 2012

Akiner Shirin, Ibrahimov Rovshan, Huseynov Ariz, 'Interregional cooperation in Eurasia: Transport and Logistic projects as an accelerator of Integration within and between the Black sea region, the South Caucasus and Central Asia", Special double issue, Vol.9-10, September 2013

Sikri Rajeev, Challenge & Strategy, Sage, India, 2009

Togan Isenbike, "Twenty Years After : New Histories Emerging", in Sengupta Anita, Chatterjee Suchandana, Sushmita Bhattacharya, ed. *Eurasia Twenty Years After*, Shipra Publishers 2012 pp.53-61

Recommendations

➢ The Eurasian region has immense geopolitical and economic significance for India especially in the context of energy potential, connectivity and civilizational linkages. Therefore, India needs to be more proactive in maintaining the relationship with the countries of this region which can work as a bridge between Europe and Asia and can help to improve cooperation and connectivity between them.

➢ India should re-invigorate intense political engagement and continue the search for newer ways for improving the economic cooperation. The relationship should be multi-dimensional in nature.

➢ India should explore the possibility of signing the *Comprehensive Economic Cooperation Agreement* (CECA) and should be able to involve itself in the Customs Union of Russia, Belarus and Kazakhstan, to improve the connectivity and trade and economic cooperation with the Eurasian States.

➢ India should expand the cooperation in areas like Information technology sector, in pharmaceuticals and in the management contracts. All these sectors do not require physical connectivity and can also add to India's efforts to diversify its relationship.

➢ India can also become a member of *Central Asia's Regional Economic Cooperation* (CAREC) as an important multilateral platform, where, India can influence the activities of CAREC by being part of the institution.

➢ India should also seriously consider enhancing civil nuclear cooperation with both Russia and Kazakhstan.

➢ There should be an active cooperation over issues of common interest including combatting terrorism, drug trafficking and on the capacity building and on human resource development sectors.

➢ In the energy Sector, there is also a need to explore the untapped natural resources and try to develop more potential energy projects.

➢ In the energy sector India could also focus on having *production sharing agreements* (PSAs) both in hydrocarbon and hydroelectricity sectors. (For example in Khatun region in the south of Tajikistan there is said to have large deposits of gas which is still unexplored. Indo-Tajik joint initiatives could help in exploring the vast opportunity that exists in the region). India's offer to assist Tajikistan in rehabilitating Vorzob could also become a positive step in expanding and strengthening cooperation in the energy sector. Energy swap agreements needs to be studied carefully to get correct details as this can also be developed as another important element of energy cooperation.

➢ One of the major challenges of India's engagement with these countries is the issue of connectivity. The land routes passing through geographically and politically hostile terrain and lack of direct surface transport routes have prevented the realisation of true potential for the economic relationship. Therefore, it is very important to look for the viable connectivity options. India's commitment for increasing connectivity with the region can be made by contributing towards its infrastructure.

➤ There is a need to improve the inadequate banking and financial services, remove the discrimination in insurance coverage in quality control concerns and improve the brand promotion activities. All these issues and concerns needs to be addressed by the government sector and remove the hurdles to improve the relationship.

➤ Efforts should be made to realize the true potential of the connectivity and start the smooth regular operations through International North South Transport Corridor (INSTC).

➤ Greater development of the *Silk Route* strategy, formulation of various joint task forces can be considered seriously. Regional countries should collaborate genuinely with Afghanistan to maintain stability in the region.

➤ Greater people to people contact and information flow is essential at the time when new democratic institutions have started growing in the Eurasian region.

Future Scenarios: Toward 2025

Future Scenarios have been developed to widen perspectives and explore uncertain aspects of the future of the region. These scenarios could indirectly foretell a possible range of the probable future as also help to seize new opportunities.

Scenario One

By 2025, there is a possibility of inflow of foreign direct investment in the Eurasian region outside the energy sector however; failure to diversify Eurasian region's economy could well lead to the 'petro-state phenomenon', leading to huge income inequality, capital flight and social tensions.

Scenario Two

Eurasian states are likely to be challenged by the twin pressures of growing population and a lack of arable land and water resources. The economic and demographic challenges can negatively impact the environment, compounding the current degradation caused by the high rates of 'dirty' resource extraction. Also, States with limited supplies of natural resources would face challenges to develop effective service industries.

Scenario Three

Ethnic unrest in the region mostly arising due to xenophobia and economic difficulties cbould cause disturbance in the region. increasing security concerns and causing civil unrest.

Scenario Four

External Powers will continue to pursue self-centered foreign policy objectives in the region. This could give rise to aggressive nationalist political moves and create more tension.

Scenario Six

India would work closely with the Central Asian Republics bordering Afghanistan i.e. mainly Uzbekistan, Tajikistan and Kazakhstan to curb security threats emanating from Afghanistan.

Scenario Seven

Revival of the silk route will bring Europe closer to Asia. India's strong civilizational linkages would be revived along with the revival of the silk route and religious and cultural connections would allow India to use its soft power potential as a diplomatic tool to engage with the region more closely.

Scenario Eight

Development of transport corridors will improve the accessibility to the region and will also reduce the time and freight cost. This will improve trade and economic cooperation between India and Eurasian states.

Scenario Nine

India would develop close contacts with multilateral organizations currently active in the region.

Scenario Ten

Cooperation in the labour movement is expected to increase in the coming years due to labour demand & demographic fall in certain Eurasian States.

Scenario Eleven

India and China would cooperate more closely to formulate a joint policy in the Eurasian region.

Scenario Twelve

Apart from the energy and defence sector, India would intensify its cooperation with the countries of the region in the information technology, science and technology as well as in the space sectors which would help to intensify the cooperation further, increasing the information flow and people to people contact.

Bibliography

1. Andre Gunder Frank, "Re-Orient: Global Economy in the Asian Age", Berkeley, University of California Press, 1998.

2. Alan Makovsky and Sabri Sayarı, "Changing Dynamics of Turkish Foreign Policy", Washington, DC:Washington Institute for Near East Policy, 2000.

3. Arthur R. Hall, "Mackinder and the Course of Events," "Annals of the Association of American Geographers", Vol. 45, No. 2 , Jun., 1955.

4. A. L. Boyer, "Recreating the Silk Road: The Challenge of Overcoming Transaction Costs","China and Eurasia Forum Quarterly", Vol. 4, No. 4, 2006.

5. Ariel Cohen, ed, "Eursaia in Balance: The US and the Regional Power Shift", Ashgae Publishing Ltd, 2005.

6. Abbott Payson Usher, "The History of Population and Settlement in Eurasia Geographical Review", Vol. 20, No. 1, Jan., 1930.

7. Andrew Higgins, "In Central Asia, a new headache for U.S. policy", "Washington Post",August, 31, 2010.

8. Alexander Lukin, ed., "StrategiyaRossii v TsentralnoiAziiiShankhay skoiorganizatsiisotrudnichestva", Moscow, MGIMO, 2012.

9. Aris, Stephen, "Eurasian Regionalism e Shanghai Cooperation

Organization", Basingstoke,Palgrave Macmillan, 2011.

10. AcharyaAmitav and Johnston Alastair Iain, eds. "Crafting Cooperation: Regional International Institutions in Comparative Perspective", Cambridge University Press, Cambridge, 2007.

11. Adler Emmanuel and Barnett Michael, eds.,"Security Communities, Cambridge, Cambridge University Press,1998.

12. Allison Roy, "Virtual Regionalism, Regional Structures and Regime Security in Central Asia", *Central Asian Survey*, Vol. *27*, No.2, 2008.

13. Bolshaia Sovetskaia Entsiklopedia, Moscow: Sovetskaia Entsiklopediia, 1977.

14. Bruce Grant, "The captive and the gift: cultural histories of sovereignty in Russia and the Caucasus", Ithaca, Cornell University Press, 2009.

15. Bruno Coppieters, Alexei Zverev and Dmitri Trenin, "Commonwealth and Independence in Post-Soviet Eurasia", London: Frank Cass, 1998.

16. Caleb Wall, "Argorods of Western Uzbekistan: knowledge control and agriculture in Khorezm", Munster, LIT Verlag, 2008.

17. Charles King and Neil J. Mervin, "Nations Abroad: Diaspora Politics and International Relations in the Former Soviet Union", Boulder, CO: Westview Press, 1998.

18. Charles King, The Benefits of Ethnic War: Understanding Eurasia's Unrecognized States, "World Politics", Vol. 53, No. 4, Jul., 2001.

19. "Calming the Ferghana Valley: development and dialogue in the heart of Central Eurasia", Report of the Ferghana Valley

Working Group of the Center for Preventive Action, New York: The Century Foundation Press, 1999.

20. Dominique M. Haughton, Selin Sayek, NicholasC. Teebagy, "Foreign Direct Investment in the Eurasian Transition States", "Eastern European Economics", Vol. 41, No. 1, Jan. - Feb., 2003.

21. David Christian, "Inner Eurasia as a Unit of World History", "Journal of World History", Vol. 5, No. 2, Fall, 1994.

22. David W. Rivera, "Engagement, Containment, and the International Politics of Eurasia", Political Science Quarterly, Vol. 118, No. 1, Spring, 2003.

23. Dmitry Shlapentokh, "Turkey and Kyrgyzstan deepen ties", *CACI Analyst*, March 21, 2012.

24. E. Vinokurov, M. Jadraliyev and Y. Shcherbanin, "The EurAsEC Transport Corridors: Sector Report", "Eurasian Development Bank", Almaty, March 2009.

25. Edlar Ismailov and Vladimer Papava, "The Central Caucasus: Problems of Geopolitical Economy", NewYork, Nova Science Publishers, 2008.

26. Faye M. L., Mcarthur J. W., Sachs J. D., Snow T., "The Challenges Facing Landlocked Developing Countries", *Journal of Human Development*, Vol. 5, No. 1, pp-31-66, March 2004.

27. "Faultline of Conflict in Central Asia and the South Caucasus", RAND Document, RAND Publications, 2003.

28. Fioramonti Lorenzo, ed., "Regions and Crises. New Challenges for Contemporary Regionalisms", Basingstoke, Palgrave Macmillan, 2012.

29. Gulnoza Saidazimova, "Kyrgyzstan: Youth Playing Key Role in Pro-Bakiyev Political Movement", (Part I)*RFE/RL*, July 7, 2005.

30. Gulnoza Saidazimova, "Kyrgyzstan: Did Revolution Sow the Seeds of Democracy? (Part II), Prague, *RFE.RL,* April 8 2005.

31. Gregory Gleason, "Markets and Politics in Central Asia", London, Routledge, 2003.

32. Gregory Gleason, "Central Asian States: Discovering Independence", Boulder, CO, Westview Press, 1997.

33. Henry Kissinger, "Diplomacy", New York: Simon and Schuster, 1994.

34. H. Y. Malik, 'Strategic Importance of Gwadar Port', Journal of Political Studies, vol. 19ᵗʰ February, 2012.

35. "Iran will help Kyrgyzstan go down the path of democracy: Larijani", *IRNA,* October 19, 2011.

36. Idrissov E,"Great Gain, not Great Game, in Central Asia", *The Straits Times,* available at http://www.straitstimes.com/opinion/great-gain-not-great-game-in-central-asia.

37. John Anderson, "The International Politics of Central Asia," Manchester: Manchester University Press, 1997.

38. Joel I. Deichmann, AbdolrezaEshghi, Jeremy Black, "Maps and History: Constructing Images of the Past", New Haven, CT: Yale University Press,1997, p 14.

39. Joshi Nirmala, "Reconnecting India and Central Asia: Emerging Security and Economic Dimensions", Pentagon Press, 2011

40. Joaquim I. Goes, Prasad G. Thoppil, Helga R. Gomes, John T. Fasullo, "Warming of the Eurasian Landmass Is Making the Arabian Sea More Productive Science", "New Series", Vol. 308, No. 5721, Apr. 22, 2005.

41. Korkut A. Erturk, ed, "Rethinking Central Asia: Non-Eurocentric Studies in History, Social Structure and Identity",

UK: Ithaca Press, 1999.

42. K Santhanam, "Eurasian Security Matters", Allied Publishers Pvt. Ltd: New Delhi, 2010.

43. K. Kumkova, "Kyrgyzstan& Tajikistan: Disputed Border Heights Risk of Conflict", *EurasiaNet*, August 2, 2012.

44. "Kyrgyzstan closes border crossing with Tajikistan", *KyrTAg, Bishkek*, May 15, 2012.

45. .Kathleen Collins, "The Political Role of Clans in Central Asia", "Comparative Politics", Vol. 35, No. 2, Jan., 2003.

46. KazharovRustam, NurovaNargis and Safranchuk Ivan, "Energeticheskoyesotrudnichestvo vramkakhShOS", Moscow, 2012.

47. Koldunova Ekaterina, "Bezopasnost v VostochnoiAzii: Novyevyzovy",

Moscow, Navona, 2010.

48. Kremlin.ru,"Sovmestnoy ezayavleniye poitogamofitsial nogovisitav, Respubliku Indiyu", 2012.

49. Kundu Das Nivedita,"12th SCO Summit in Beijing: A View from India", Valdai Discussion Club,available at http:// valdaiclub.com/asia/44660.html.

50. LaruelleMarlene and PeyrouseSébastien, 'Regionalnyeorganizatsii v TsentralnoiAzii:kharakteristikivza imodeistviy, dilemmye ektivnosti', Report No.10, available at http://www.ucentralasia.org/downloads/UCA-IPPA-WP-10-RegionalOrganizations-Rus.pdf

51. Laruelle Marlene and PeyrouseSébastien, "Chinese Question in Central Asia: DomesticOrder, Social Change and the Chinese Factor", London, Hurst & Company, 2012.

52. Lin Gang; Garver John; Hickey Dennis and Chambers

Michael, "China's "Good Neighbor" Diplomacy: A Wolf in Sheep's Clothing?", "Asia Program Special Report", No. 126, 2005.

53. Linn Johannes, 'Central Asian Regional Integration and Cooperation: Reality or Mirage?' EDBEurasian Integration Yearbook 2012, Available at, URL http://www.brookings. edu/~/media/research/files/papers/2012/10/regional%20 integration%20and%20cooperation%20linn/10%20 regional%20integration%20and%20cooperation%20linn.pdf

54. Lukin   Alexander,   ed., "StrategiyaRossii   v TsentralnoiAziiiShankhaiskoi   organizatsiisotrudnichestva, Moscow, MGIMO, 2012.

55. Leonard A Stone, 'Research and Eurasia: geopolitical contours', "Perceptions in Journal of International Affairs", Vol 6, No 1, 2001, pp 135–150.

56. Markus Perkmann and Ngai-Ling Sum, eds, "Globalization, Regionalization and Cross Border Regions", Basingstoke, UK: Palgrave, 2002.

57. Mehdi ParviziAmineh and HenkHouweling, eds, "Central Eurasia in Global Politics: Conflict, Security, and Development", Leiden: Brill, 2004.

58. Mark Von Hagen, "Empires, Borderlands, and Diasporas: Eurasia as Anti-Paradigm for the Post-Soviet Era", in "The American Historical Review", Vol. 109, No. 2 (April 2004).

59. Mariya Y, Omelicheva Y. M.,*Nationalism and Identity Construction in Central Asia: Dimensions, Dynamics, and Directions,* Lexington Books, 2014.

60. Mehdi Parvizi Amineh, "Globalization, Geopolitics and Energy Security in Central Eurasia and the Caspian Region", The Hague: Clingendael Energy, 2003.

61. M. Emerson and E. Vinokurov, "Optimisation of Central Asian and Eurasian Trans-Continental Land Transport Corridors", EUCAM Working Paper no. 7, December 2009.

62. Manmohan Parkash, "Connecting Central Asia: A Road Map for Regional Cooperation", ADB Manila, 2006.

63. Mark Bassin, "Russia between Europe and Asia: The Ideological Construction of Geographical Space", "Slavic Review", Vol. 50, No. 1, Spring, 1991.

64. M.A.Kaw and A.A. Banday, eds., "Central Asia Introspection", Crown Press, Srinagar, 2006

65. Nacelenia Rossia, "EdzegodniyieDemographicheskieDoklad", Center Demographicheskie Chelavieka, Moscow, 1993.

66. Nicklas Norling and Niklas Swanström, "The Virtues and Potential Gains of Continental Trade in Eurasia", "Asian Survey", Vol. 47, No. 3, May - Jun., 2007.

67. Oliver Roy, "The New Central Asia: The Creation of Nations", New York: New York University Press, 2000.

68. Oskar Kayasan, "Strategic Pragmatism of Central Asian States from Global Perspectives", , "Journal of Global Strategic Management", European Research Centre, UK, 2010, December

69. "Obama administration lists Kyrgyzstan and Tajikistan as priority assistance countries in Central Asia for 2012", *AKIpress,* February 16, 2012.

70. Olga Shumylo Tapiola, "The Eurasian Customs Union: Friend or Foe of the EU?" Carnegie Papers, Carnegie Endowment for International Peace, Brussels, October 2012.

71. Pauline Jones Luong, "Institutional Change and Political Continuity in Post-Soviet Central Asia: Power, Perceptions, and Pacts", Cambridge: Cambridge University Press, 2002.

72. Paul Titus and Nina Swidler, "Knights, Not Pawns: Ethno-Nationalism and Regional Dynamics, "International Journal of Middle East Studies", Vol. 32, No. 1 Feb., 2000.

73. P.S. Paramjit Sahai ed., "India-Eurasia: The Way Ahead", Chandigarh: CRRID, 2008.

74. Pabst, Adrian, *Central Eurasia in the Emerging Global Balance of Power*, American Foreign Policy Interests, Volume 31, Number 3, May 2009.

75. QoraboyevIkboljon, "From Central Asian Regional Integration to Eurasian Integration Space: the Changing Dynamics of Post-Soviet Regionalism", "EDB Eurasian Integration Yearbook 2010."

76. Robert D. Kaplan, 'The coming anarchy', "The Atlantic Monthly", 1994.

77. Robert M. Cutler, 'The Caspian energy conundrum', "Journal of International Affairs", Vol 21, No 2, 2003, pp 89–102.

78. Richard Weitz, "Global Security Watch Russia: A Reference Handbook", "World Politics Review", February 10, 2009.

79. R. Pomfret, "Trade and Transport in Central Asia", "Emerging Markets Forum", Centennial Group report, Washington DC, January 2010.

80. RovshanIbrahimov, "Azerbaijan Energy Strategy and the Importance of the Divercification of Exported Transport Routes", Journal ofQafqaz University, No 29, 2010.

81. RovshanIbrahimov, "Azerbaijan`s Energy History and Policy: From Past till Our Days", in RovshanIbrahimov, ed., "Energy and Azerbaijan: History, Strategy and Cooperation", SAM, Baku, 2013.

82. Robert M. Cutler, 'The complexity of Central Eurasia', Central Eurasian Studies Review, Vol 3, No 1, 2004, p 3.

83. Richard Lugar, "Energy Security: Cause for Cooperation or Competition"?90th Anniversary Leadership Series, The Brooking Institution, 2006.

84. Shiping Tang, "Economic Integration in Central Asia: The Russian and Chinese Relationship", Asian Survey, Vol. 40, No. 2 Mar. – April, 2000.

85. Sergey Luzyanin, "Central Asia in Trilateral Cooperation: Regional Potential and Resources of SCO", "China Report", 2007.

86. Scott C. Levi and Ron Sela, eds. "Islamic Central Asia: an anthology of historical sources",Bloomington, Indiana University Press, 2010.

87. Sachdeva Gulshan, India's Attitude towards China's Growing Influence in Central Asia, "China and Eurasia Forum Quarterly", Volume 4, No. 3, 2006.

88. Starr Fedrric, "The New Central Asia", *YouTube,* available at https://www.youtube.com/watch?v=tIde2QSDwZk.

89. S. Akiner ed., "The Caspian: Politics, Energy, Security", Routledge, Curzon, London/NY, 2004

90. S. Akiner, "The Shanghai Cooperation Organisation: A Networking Organisation for a Networking World", Global Strategy Forum Paper, London, July 2010.

91. S. F. Starr ed., "The New Silk Road: Transport and Trade in Greater Central Asia", Central Asia-Caucasus Institute Silk Road Studies Program, John Hopkins University-SAIS, Washington DC/Uppsala University, Uppsala, 2007.

92. Shumaila Andleeb, "Pakistan, Kyrgyzstan agree on reviving four-nation trade pact", APP, March 15, 2011.

93. Tomohiko Uyama, "Empire, Islam and Politics in Central Eurasia", "Slavic Eurasian Studies", No. 14. Sapporo, Hokkaido

University, 2007.

94. Vladimir V. Pitul'ko, "Ancient Humans in Eurasian Arctic Ecosystems: Environmental Dynamics and Changing Subsistence World Archaeology", Vol. 30, No. 3, Arctic Archaeology, Feb., 1999.

95. William Fierman, ed, "Soviet Central Asia: The Failed Transformation", Boulder, CO: Westview Press, 1991.

96. Walter Kegö, "Internationally Organized Crime The Escalation of Crime within the Global Economy", Central Eurasian Studies Review, 2008.

97. Walter Pincus, "Bethesda-based development firm gets Kyrgyzstan contract", "Washington Post", October 24, 2010.

98. Washington-based Silk Road Newline on February 15, 2012. Executive Budget Summary released by the Department of State said "The FY 2012 request prioritizes assistance for the Kyrgyz Republic to support the new Government's efforts to reform core institutions, law enforcement, and increase economic opportunities."

99. Zh. Zharmagambetova, L. Flake, "Kazakhstan: Grain and Feed Update", USDA Foreign Agricultural Service Global Agricultural Information Network (GAIN) Report, 25 July 2012.

100. Zbigniew Brzezinski, "A Geo-strategy for Eurasia", "Foreign Affairs", Vol. 76, No. 5, Sep. - Oct., 1997.

Index

A

Amudarya 5

Ashkelon- Eilat pipeline 82

Asian Development Bank xv, 28, 50, 66, 72, 110

Asian Land Transport Infrastructure Development xv, 59

Ayni Airbase 24. *See also* Gissar Air Base

B

Baikal-Amur Mainline xv, 58

Baku-Tbilisi-Ceyhan xv, 39, 40, 57, 81

Bandar Abbas 60, 62, 73, 80

Black Sea Economic Cooperation xv, 56

Bolshevik Revolution 15

BrahMos 17

Brazil-Russia-India-China xi, xv, 9, 20, 89, 104, 105, 106, 107, 108, 114

C

Caspian Sea 7, 9, 36, 40, 56, 60, 61, 62, 81

Center for Joint Warfare Studies ix, xiii

Central Asian Regional Economic Cooperation xi, xv, 89, 110, 111, 114, 122

Central Asian Republics xv, 4, 23, 24, 34, 114, 125

Central Eurasia 14, 20, 86, 87

Chabahar port 59

Chandrayaan II 17

Chekalov Aircraft Plant 24

Collective Security Treaty Organisation xv, 95, 115

Commonwealth of Independent States xv, 30, 95, 115

Comprehensive Convention on International Terrorism xv, 39

Comprehensive Economic Cooperation Agreement xv, 121

Index

Author

Nivedita Das Kundu, PhD, in International Studies, is Senior Research Advisor with United Service Institution of India. Her research expertise focusses on geopolitics, geo-economics, foreign policy, multilateral organisations, border issues, migration and strategic dimensions of security. She has also worked on WMD issues. Dr. Nivedita has worked extensively on Silk Route and transport corridor issues and concerns. She is a recipient of prestigious "**Pushkin Medal**", She has authored and edited books, Monographs on "Russia and it's Near Abroad: Strategic Dynamics and Implications", "Baku-Tbilisi-Kars Railroads: Iron Ground for the Silk Road", "Role of Russia in SCO: Possibilities and Challenges", "Russia-India-China: Evolution of Geopolitical Strategic Trends", "India-Russia Strategic Partnership: Challenges and Prospects", "India-Azerbaijan: The Silk Route Connection", "China's One Belt One Road: Initiatives, Challenges and Prospects", and published research articles on her area of research in India and abroad. She is a recipient of various prestigious fellowships including DAAD (Germany), CIMO (EU), RAS (Russia), ADA (Azerbaijan), ICSSR (India). She has worked with prestigious Government Think Tanks & Universities in India and abroad.